*Characters in Search
of Their Author*

Characters

in Search
of Their

Author

The Gifford Lectures
Glasgow
1999–2000

RALPH McINERNY

University of Notre Dame Press
Notre Dame, Indiana

Manufactured in the United States of America

Library of Congress Cataloging-in-Publication Data
McInerny, Ralph M.
Characters in search of their author / Ralph McInerny.
p.   cm. — (The Gifford Lectures ; 1999–2000)
Includes bibliographical references and index.
ISBN 0-268-02261-5 (hardcover : alk. paper)
1. Natural theology.   I. Title.   II. Series.
BL182 .M37   2000
210—dc21
00-010904

∞ *This book was printed on acid-free paper.*

for

M A R I O E N R I Q U E S A C C H I

Querido amigo

Nox nocti indicat scientiam

Ps. 18*

---

* Sed tempus noctis est tempus meditationis propter quietem; et ideo in quiete noctis homo meditatur, et adinvenit multa ex quibus fit sciens, et ideo est tempus scientiae.— St. Thomas

Though giant rains put out the sun,
Here stand I for a sign,
Though earth be filled with waters dark
My cup is filled with wine.

Tell to the trembling priests that here
Under the deluge rod,
One nameless, tattered, broken man
Stood up and drank to God.

G. K. CHESTERTON

Contents

Preface

After I received the invitation to give a series of Gifford Lectures at the University of Glasgow, I perused the volumes of previous lecturers with renewed interest. It soon became apparent to me that the usual procedure was this. The lecturer delivered his lectures at the appointed time and then a period of varying length, often years, intervened during which the lectures were prepared for publication. Since I would be fulfilling my assignment when I had reached the allotted three score and ten, I felt it would be hubristic to assume that I might be given adequate time to follow this procedure. Accordingly, I decided to reverse it.

I wrote a book which bears the title *Praeambula Fidei*, a philosophical book of the usual kind, full of arguments, exegesis, and documentation. Its length would have made reading it in Glasgow out of the question, and its style would have guaranteed a soporific experience to those who came to the lecture hall. Furthermore, Lord Gifford intended the lectures to be intelligible to a cultivated but non-professional audience and, while the general culture of Scotland permits a more demanding style than would be advisable elsewhere, the lectures I gave struck a lighter note than the book to which I have referred.

In order to underscore the different key in which I am playing variations on my theme, I gave the actual lectures a title of their own. Those who find them somewhat swift in places, arguments being suggested rather than developed, may perhaps find what they want in *Praeambula Fidei* when it appears. For in this at least I will mimic the usual procedure, publishing the lectures I actually gave before publishing the book on which, sometimes remotely, they are based.

I must thank Professor Alexander Broadie and the other members of the Gifford committee of the University of Glasgow for the great honor they paid me in asking me to give these lectures. My stay in Glasgow was intellectually stimulating and socially entertaining, and I look back on it with pleasure and gratitude. I would be remiss indeed if I did not say how enormously helpful Mrs. Eileen Reynolds was in seeing after the innumerable details involved in making a visiting scholar feel welcome. She and Mrs. Alice Osberger, Administrative Assistant of the Jacques Maritain Center at the University of Notre Dame, joined forces, pooling their formidable resources of efficiency. I am grateful to them both. To Sir Jimmy Armour, with whom I played Royal Troon, many thanks for his generosity and patience. Finally, I want to thank Stanley Jaki, O.S.B., for sending me a copy of his history of the Gifford Lectures, *Lord Gifford and His Lectures,* an indispensable book.

PART ONE

Whatever Happened to Natural Theology?

Personal Prejudice
and Natural Theology

West of Agrigento on a narrow country road can be found the house in which Luigi Pirandello lived as a boy. It is now a tourist attraction, operated by the government. The house overlooks the Mediterranean and as one gazes seaward from the house an old leafless tree seems to search the azure air like an arthritic hand. Embedded in that dead tree are the ashes of the author of *Six Characters in Search of an Author*.

The play was written in 1921 and bears the mark of the modern—art fascinated with its own medium, becoming its own subject. But Pirandello's play, by separating the characters from the actors, and both from the author, underscores the inescapable dependence of both—on Luigi Pirandello. Of course, to be a character entails an author of its being, so however successful or unsuccessful the search, the quest is predicated on the possibility of success.

Dramatic characters stand in a complicated relation to real agents. We follow their doings just because in some way they stand for us, and the intelligibility or lack of it on the stage is a metaphor of our lives. Hamlet will have them well treated because "they are the abstracts and brief chronicles of the time" (2.2). It has been said that life is a book in which we set out to write one story and end by writing another. Deflective surprises are due to chance or, as men have thought from time immemorial, to another author in whose drama we are but players. A play within a play. How can we not be in search of our author?

Lectures in natural theology have a distant air about them, as if they dealt with matters so abstruse that ordinary folk could not be interested or perhaps even follow what is being said. The formal effort to construct proofs with an eye to showing that God's existence is as inescapable as the premises that precede is indeed a difficult matter and one who lifted his voice in the average pub to recite such a proof is unlikely to win a host of adherents. If he does, we will suspect that something other than cogency is involved.

The Greeks, from whom we have all learned philosophy, made knowledge of the divine the mark of the wise man, and the acquisition of wisdom the task of a lifetime. The neophyte was not ready to ask the ultimate questions—and the existence of God is surely an ultimate question. A lengthy curriculum had to be followed and anywhere along the way one might stop—with mathematics, with natural science—and not continue to philosophy's term. Or be diverted altogether by pressing practical concerns.

But if that is the case with the elite, what must be said of those— the vast majority of mankind—who are not enrolled in the Academy or Lyceum? If there is a God who is the author of us all, awareness of his existence should surely not be restricted to a few. How could any character in the human drama fail to search in some way for his author?

We are to God as characters are to their author. It may be a violation of the assumptions of art for imaginary characters to go in search of the writer who made them. But for us it is all but inevitable that, however momentarily, we feel ourselves to be part of a vast cosmic drama and our thoughts turn to the author, not merely of our roles, but of our existence.

Natural theology is one version of that quest. It is my task, under the auspices of the will of Adam Gifford, at the invitation of the Principal and the Gifford committee, to speak on the topic of natural theology. I have been given ten lectures in which to do so, a rare privilege. The assumption can safely be made that a lecturer has given some thought to his subject before he rises to speak. For an old philosopher, it is difficult to remember exactly when the subject of natural theology first swam before his mind's eye. Any philosopher will, when he hears the phrase "natural theology," feel something stir within him, a reaction either positive or negative. [I will simply decree that anyone indifferent in the matter does not count as a philosopher.] My own reaction is a positive stirring. Like Adam Gifford, I think that there is such a thing as natural theology.

What Is It?

Natural theology, as I use the phrase—and this is not an idiosyncratic use of it—means the philosophical discipline which proves that God exists and that he has certain attributes. It is theology because it is concerned with God, and it is natural because it makes use of our natural powers unaided by any supernatural revelation. Natural theology is thus distinct from Christian theology which assumes as true what God has revealed to us about himself.

My Predisposition

Whence comes my benevolent attitude toward natural theology? For one thing, I am a Catholic—a contented and grateful one, I might add. The long tradition of the Church in this matter culminated at the First Vatican Council where it was declared to be of faith (*de fide*) that God can be known by our natural powers independent of faith, grace, or revelation. This will seem to be a paradoxical situation, perhaps: a dogmatic declaration that dogma is not necessary for one to know that God exists. But anyone responsive to the dogma already holds that God exists on faith. This must apply to someone else. But why then does the Church bother with the subject? A long story that, the latest chapter of which is *Fides et ratio*, an encyclical issued a year ago.

As a believer I accept on faith that God exists. As a Catholic, I take it to be of faith that God's existence can be known apart from faith. But I am, allegedly, a philosopher. My situation, as just summarized, would in the eyes of some disqualify me for philosophizing. A moment ago I was reading anyone indifferent to natural theology out of the ranks, now I seem to have described myself in such a way that I must myself be ostracized.

The objection is that one who as a matter of religion believes in God is in no position to discuss the question of God's existence, because he has already begged that question. As a philosopher, who is expected to follow the argument wherever it leads him, he should have an open mind. But the believer does not philosophize in the expectation that his faith will shortly be undermined. Is it a condition for doing natural theology, or any other philosophical task, that we come to it without any antecedent convictions? It is a rather widespread conviction among professional philosophers that natural theology cannot be brought to a successful term. Nor is this attitude absent from the ranks of believers.

ANTIPATHETIC BELIEVERS

There are many Christians, some of them are my colleagues, who as Protestants are appalled at the very notion of natural theology. For them it is an abomination that sinful man should seek to bridge the gap between himself and the deity by way of syllogisms.

Believers who are affirmatively disposed and believers who are negatively disposed toward natural theology will soon be exchanging snippets of Scripture to justify their attitude. I will cite Romans 1:19; my interlocutor will cite Colossians 2:8, to the effect that we should not be led astray by philosophy. On the sidelines, following this with amusement, is a third party who is not a believer and who sees this battle of believers as a sign that neither party can engage in philosophizing, properly understood. But let us take a look at this third party.

THE *SOI-DISANT* STANDARD PHILOSOPHER

Our observer is not indifferent to the matter of natural theology. Let us say that he would come to this study with the antecedent conviction that proofs of God's existence are impossible because God does not exist. And, even if God did exist, it would be impossible for us to know it.

This fellow admittedly gains acceleration from the *zeitgeist*. There seems little doubt that philosophy is all but definitionally agnostic now, if not matter-of-factly atheist. The philosopher has become a thoroughly secularized fellow, most likely someone who in the mists of memory believed but has long since put away the things of a child, thanks to philosophy. How would he describe himself as a philosopher?

More or less as pure reason. Questions come to his attention from he knows not where; in any case, their provenance is irrelevant. He ponders the question, he considers solutions, he weighs the possibilities, he makes his dispassionate judgment. He is for all practical purposes anonymous.

Now you and I know this fellow. We have argued with him. Does this disembodied portrait fit him? On the question of natural theology—is there a God, are we and the world his effects?—his mind is not a blank slate. Whatever his condition might have been when he signed up for a course called Introduction to Philosophy, now he has an antecedent attitude toward the possible outcome of the question. He does not think God's existence has ever been proved. Logically, this does not prove God to be non-existent, but he will not therefore put the question on hold. We know how he would fill out prying questionnaires. Religion? None. Meaning he does not think there is a God.

My Generalization

My point in drawing attention to these obvious yet somehow forgettable facts is both to tell you that I take up my task in the firm prephilosophical conviction, thanks to my Christian faith, that it can be done, and that my having pre-philosophical antecedent convictions is not unique, but is simply a variation on the common fact that everyone comes to every inquiry with antecedent convictions. If having antecedent beliefs disqualified one from philosophy, there could be no philosophers.

All philosophers have acquired a lengthy personal history before they even begin the study of philosophy. The effort to rid oneself of all that baggage—for some centuries now taken to be the first philosophical task—is an acknowledgment of its presence. Nor it is ever completely discarded. Item. Etienne Gilson's detection of all kinds of covert scholasticism in Descartes himself, who thought he had bade adieu to all that.

My intention is not to return an insult for an insult. *Tu quoque*, as it were. Reflection makes it clear that everyone thinks out of a very complicated personal background, one that affects what questions he enter-tains, the expectations he has of possible answers, and doubtless causes him to give short shrift to lines of thought which disturb those an-tecedents. Imagine how difficult it would be for someone with the *zeit-geist* in his sails to follow with sympathy the effort to prove the existence of God. And of course, think of how the believer would react to any at-tempt to show that talk of God is meaningless.

Thus far, then, three points:

1. I take up the topic of natural theology in the expectation that it can successfully fulfill my expectations of it. This stems from my reli-gious belief.
2. Nonetheless, many fellow Christians hold the opposite attitude to-ward natural theology.
3. It is not only believers who have such antecedent convictions: everyone does.

OBJECTION

All this might be admitted as a matter of course but objection may be taken to my passing so lightly over the fact that the modern turn in philosophy was aimed precisely at overcoming such antecedent atti-tudes—common sense, the confusions and errors into which the mind has fallen, received and unexamined opinion of various kinds. What was needed was a severe application of the Socratic maxim: *The unex-amined life is not worth living.* (The novelist Peter DeVries pointed out that many students would prefer the unexamined to the examined life, but no matter.) A cold eye must be cast on what is given and presup-posed—on tradition, on common sense—with nothing being admitted that does not pass the test of methodic doubt. Antecedent attitudes are to be overcome, not appealed to for guidance, however covert. This drama was played out again and again in modern times. It therefore must seem disingenuous of me to invoke the given as, well, given.

This is an important objection, and one to which I must shortly return. But for the moment I want to dwell on the special condition of the believing philosopher.

CHRISTIAN PHILOSOPHY

Etienne Gilson, in his ebullient Gifford lectures, *The Spirit of Medieval Philosophy*, celebrated what he called the Christian Philosophy of the Middle Ages, just at the time that his fellow historian, Emile Brehier, in an article that asked *Y-a-t-il une philosophie chrétienne?*, was suggesting a negative answer. For Brehier it seemed obvious that believers, for whom the great questions of philosophy had already received their answers, could scarcely go about seeking those same answers. They were already committed. They could not follow the argument wherever it might take them.

This article of Brehier's set off, as you may know, a tremendous reaction among believers. In the Thirties, just about every Continental Catholic philosopher of renown—or soon to be renowned—published a little book on Christian philosophy. The meeting of the *Société Thomiste* at Juvisy in 1933 was devoted to the question. There was anything but unanimity. The disagreement between the eminent medievalists Mandonnet and Gilson is particularly instructive. For Gilson it was simply a matter of historical fact that during the ages of faith certain philosophical truths had either been broached for the first time—e.g., the concept of person—or had come more sharply into focus—e.g., the nature of the first cause—within the ambiance of the faith. Whether or not they would have been developed without that influence, the historical fact remained.

Mandonnet impatiently pointed out that an argument was either a philosophical argument or a theological one—dependent on faith—and that Gilson was confusing philosophy with theology.

This theme took on new life twenty years ago in the United States when the Society of Christian Philosophers was formed, and once more a variety of positions, not all of them compatible, were developed by those identifying themselves as Christian philosophers.

What is incontestable is that religious belief influences the philosophizing of Christian philosophers, unless they are schizophrenic. It is safe to say that no Christian philosopher sits down at his desk in the expectation that he will rise from it convinced that God does not exist, that the human soul is mortal, or that we will not be held accountable for our deeds. His life would make no sense if these were false. Does that preclude his asking whether there are sound arguments for the existence of God and the immortality of the soul?

While the case of the believer is indeed distinctive, it is a mistake to regard it as unique. For many, philosophizing is an activity that has become totally secularized. If the thinker had religious faith, he has put it aside. Indeed, it would seem professionally gauche if he were to admit to religious faith. The working assumption is that anyone who uses his mind seriously must put aside religious beliefs.

Say that is a fair picture of the profession. If philosophers were polled on the question whether it is possible to prove the existence of God, the vast majority would likely say no. Some few of them would do so on the basis of extended examination of attempts to prove God's existence. But for many this conviction is simply there, breathed in with the atmosphere of secularized philosophy. This is the antecedent conviction of many, perhaps most, professional philosophers. If you ask a class of undergraduates, neophytes in philosophy, if they think it possible to prove God's existence, almost none will answer in the affirmative. (I speak as a professor of philosophy in a Catholic university.) Does this disqualify them from considering such proofs? Are professional philosophers who antecedently think it impossible to prove that God exists *toto coelo* different from the believing philosopher who thinks it possible?

RELATIVISM?

You will perhaps be feeling dismay. I began by admitting my own antecedent attitude toward the project of natural philosophy. I asked if this disqualified me from going on with my task. Then I suggested that everyone is in a similar position. Nonetheless, believers differ among themselves on the possibility of natural theology, so an affirmative attitude does not seem entailed by Christian faith. Perhaps one has to be a Catholic, or a member of a diminishing subset of Catholics, to have such antecedent confidence. But now, after seeming to exempt him, I am back suggesting that the non-believing philosopher, like the believing philosopher, has antecedent convictions on the matter of natural theology which ought to disqualify him as well.

But your dismay could go to the implications of what I am doing. If everyone's philosophizing is influenced by antecedent convictions, philosophy will seem to be merely the formation of reasons for what we already hold to be true. One's philosophical position will reflect his antecedent attitudes. Antecedent attitudes differ. Therefore, the radical diversity among philosophers is not a function of argument but of subjectivity.

Such considerations do indeed explain why agreement is so hard to come by in philosophy. Philosophers are regularly astounded by colleagues who resist what seem to their proponents to be airtight arguments. But if agreement is difficult, it is not impossible.

A philosopher's antecedent attitudes will influence the questions he finds attractive, they will lead him to expect one result rather than another from his inquiry, and they may cause him to think he has a good argument when he hasn't. This is not a peculiarity of one species of philosopher. It is an ineluctably common fact about philosophers.

Here is my stay against a chaotic relativism. Whatever the personal reasons for pursuing a given question, whatever expectations one might have as to its solution, the position he arrives at and the arguments he formulates are appraisable by criteria which float free of the various and conflicting antecedent attitudes of philosophers.

I simply assert this now. I intend to address it more thoroughly in the sequel.

The Advantage of Christian Philosophy

But I would not want you to think that the condition of the non-believing and of the believing philosopher were in every way the same. Many believers, under the influence of the current prejudices of the profession, accept the judgment that they are somehow suspect and anomalous. And even if the kind of argument I am suggesting can be made, they would go on regarding themselves as somehow handicapped by their religious faith. This leads to the distressing spectacle of believers proceeding as if they did not believe, taking a working skepticism to be a condition of doing philosophy. But a faith thus set aside may not be there when one goes back for it.

My view is that the religious believer is at a tremendous advantage in philosophy.

The reason is that his antecedent attitude is not based on hearsay, the idols of the tribe, what the most respected thinkers hold, etc., but on the Word of God. The believer holds as true what God has revealed to be true and has the sanction of God himself for them. Collective human reason may be fallible, but God is not. That is significantly different from holding something on the basis of human trust, on ordinary human faith. I am speaking of antecedent attitudes of course.

No doubt the skeptical secularist finds this steady confidence in the range of reason annoying. Perhaps he can take some comfort in this frank statement of a believing philosopher's belief that his antecedents are an advantage, not an impediment, to doing philosophy. His worst fears are realized.

A CORNER OF THE VEIL

A recent French theological thriller turns on the impact of a proof for the existence of God which is completely irresistible and carries with it none of the difficulties associated with the traditional proofs, whether cosmological or ontological.[1] The novel explores the social effects such a proof would have. The proof itself is not given in the novel, as it happens—doubtless a wise literary decision—but its characteristics as described are crucial for the story. Six handwritten pages contain a proof so compelling and immediately intelligible that simply to read the pages is to drive forever from the mind any doubt that there is a God.

Among the political assumptions threatened by the proof is the toleration of different views. Modern society tries not to give the believer any advantage over the non-believer and vice versa. This is grounded on the belief that such questions cannot be rationally resolved. But, given those six pages, it now becomes impossible to deny the existence of God and whole bureaucracies and legal provisions and the courts and lawyers and functionaries employed by them become obsolete overnight. How could those who reject the obvious be taken seriously?

1. Laurence Cossé, *A Corner of the Veil,* trans. Linda Asher (New York: Scribner, 1999).

Already one can see that the novel conflates theism and religious belief. Indeed, the proof comes to the attention of members of a religious order patterned on the Jesuits and the final scenes of the novel are played out in Rome. It may seem churlish to insist that a proof of God's existence leaves the truth of Christianity an open question, but if the proof is supposed to include the mysteries of the Christian faith, there is a fundamental confusion at the heart of the novel. What would an irresistible proof of the Trinity look like? Since the proof is kept off-stage, there is no way to tell whether this confusion is contained in the proof. But it is, alas, necessary for the novel that the proof be thought to make any ecclesiastical mediation between man and God otiose since now this must seem like needing an authority for $2+2=4$. One can, of course, waive such niceties and enjoy the novel, and I hope you will, but its confusion provides an occasion for an important and final preliminary point.

The task of natural theology is to arrive at some truths about God—that he exists, that he is one, intelligent, cause of all else, etc.—but no matter how wildly successful it is, there is an infinite distance between its truths and the Christian mysteries. The truths the natural theologian establishes by argument were previously accepted on faith by the believing philosopher. But among the things he believes is that the crucial and distinctive truths of Christianity cannot be established by such proofs. God's existence and some of his attributes can be proved by beginning with truths in the public domain, those common truths that everyone who has standard and unimpaired natural cognitive equipment can be taken to know. If the mysteries of the faith were provable like that, it is conceivable that someone might hit upon them simply by carrying on in the usual philosophical way. Once more, the believer as believer holds the opposite, and of course no such proofs have ever been fashioned. The believer holds that it is only thanks to God's mercy that we have been informed of the divinity as well as humanity of Christ and his crucial role in our salvation. There is something grotesque in the suggestion that a chemical analysis of the Eucharist should be able to settle claims of Transubstantiation, or that Christ's DNA would provide a basis for testing his claim to divinity.

The difference between truths held ultimately on the basis of what everyone knows and truths held on the authority of the one revealing is total. Natural theology does not establish the truth of Christianity, and the truths it does yield do not bring the mind a millimeter closer to holding the truths of the Trinity, Resurrection, and Incarnation on any basis other than the authority of God.

PERORATION

Please forgive the autobiographical testimony in this first lecture, but reticence here can only give aid and comfort to the secularist conception of philosophy. I thought it wise to lay my own cards on the table from the outset. As a Catholic, I am antecedently disposed to think that the tasks of natural theology can be successfully accomplished. Holding this at the present time is counter-cultural, at least so far as philosophical culture goes. One might be more shaken by this if the present state of philosophy were different than it is. In my next lecture I will attempt a barefoot trip over the terrain of modern philosophy that takes one to a contemporary situation where philosophers are urged to become "strong poets." Apart from the fact that this is a libel on poetry, it is an admission of the ultimate bankruptcy of philosophy understood as the quest for truth.

As a believer, I am proud of the fact that the Church has stood athwart the path modern philosophy has taken. Her warnings have been frequent and to the point, as even non-believers have come to see. Like Jacques Maritain early in this century, one becomes convinced that the appropriate stance of the proponent of natural theology, to say nothing of the believer, is to be *Antimoderne*. Now we witness the irony that it is the Church—I think of John Paul II's recent encyclical *Fides et ratio*, Faith and Reason—that comes to the defense of reason and its capacity to know the truth. Why should the Church bother? Because the faith is compatible with reason and is its fulfillment, though a fulfillment reason could not achieve on its own. But what reason can achieve is presupposed by the faith. And as believers we know that some knowledge of God is possible on the basis of reason alone. This is the role of natural theology.

OCTOBER 26, 1999

Friends and Foes of Natural Theology

Having addressed some subjective difficulties that arise when natural theology is to be undertaken, I turn now to the subject itself. Is it possible for human beings, relying solely on their native cognitive equipment, to come to knowledge of God without any essential dependence on religious revelation? Whatever one's antecedent disposition toward the question, answers proposed to it must be appraised by criteria which are not merely the prejudices of some.

The antecedent dispositions of the individual are one thing. The wider context in which they are formed another. No individual is simply a product of a culture, indistinguishable from his fellows. But there are broad cultural contexts within which the question of natural theology is viewed. One of them is the ambiance of professional philosophers. No one is born a philosopher, but whatever the postulant brings to the door of philosophy, when he enters he will find himself in an established atmosphere. In this lecture I shall trace with irresponsible simplicity the fortune of natural theology among philosophers.

I have portrayed the present time, as one millennium comes to an end and another begins, as hostile to the question of natural theology. Professional philosophers, by and large, are at best agnostic with respect to the question of God's existence. This makes the pursuit of natural theology more difficult. Only a century ago, the relation between God and philosophy was thought to be too easily established.

A Plea for Difficulty

Johannes Climacus, the Kierkegaardian pseudonym who deals with philosophy, describes himself of a Sunday afternoon, enjoying a cigar in the park and thinking how easy current philosophy had made things. The great tasks of life were discussed with abstract wordiness, but the message was simple. Philosophy had at last arrived at the point, or very near the point, where the question that chiefly interested Søren Kierkegaard, Climacus's creator—What does it mean to be a Christian?—had lost its difficulty. Both Climacus and his creator are surprised by this. They think the question is as difficult as it has ever been, if not more so. So too with the questions presupposed by it. "The reason we have forgotten what it is to be a Christian is that we have forgotten what it is to be a man." Philosophers had described themselves as a bodiless *res cogitans*. Climacus puffs on his cigar. A resolution forms. Let others try to make life easier in virtue of abstract thought. He will bend his efforts to making life more difficult.

Kierkegaard issues a caveat against accepting the wrong kind of help in such matters. Many had embraced the Hegelian reconstruction of Christianity.[1] Kierkegaard ridiculed the notion that by subsuming Christianity into the enterprise of Thought, it could be made fully intelligible. "Philosophy is the truth of religion," Hegel had said. All puzzles about religious thought could at last be solved. But Kierkegaard saw that when Christianity is fed into the Hegelian system, something very different emerges. There are protectors whose ministrations are fatal to the protégé.

The question then is not so much whether or not philosophy is hospitable to natural theology, but rather what are the conditions of its hospitality. An outright rejection of natural theology is preferable to the *laissez-passer* sometimes given. The dominant secular attitude of professional philosophers is, alas, incontestable. Nonetheless, it might be said that the dark clouds shifted long ago and that no more obstacles stand in the path of natural theology.[2]

---

1. See *Fides et ratio,* n. 46.
2. I will discuss later the Pickwickian passport offered by one understanding of Wittgenstein, as well as the even more equivocal ones issued by Nietzsche and Richard Rorty.

If that were true, then my stance would become Kierkegaardian. I will say things contrary both to those who think that the obstacles to natural theology raised by secular philosophy are gone, and to those who regard the impossibility of natural theology as received opinion. The vagaries of the discipline over the past 2,500 years are instructive.

A Barefoot Trip

To begin in the middle: it would of course be historically false to say that modern philosophy and the rejection of natural theology go hand in hand. Indeed, the Cartesian turn, the subjective turn, can be said to have ushered in a happy time for natural theology. Contemporary philosophers must not read back into the origins of modern philosophy their own agnosticism. The only way Descartes could get out of his mind, once he imagined it possible that he could be utterly mistaken that there is an external world, was by way of a proof for the existence of God as guarantor of the validity of his knowledge. It would be too much to say that, for Descartes, proving the existence of God was a mere bagatelle, but it was soon done. Descartes, methodically reduced to a thinking subject unsure that any of the objects of thought had real counterparts, is delivered from his solipsism by the conviction that the idea of God is one he could not have fashioned himself. He is not its cause. Its cause is outside his mind, is indeed God himself. God becomes the guarantor of the reliability of Descartes's senses and the world, albeit upside-down, is back again.[3]

Descartes was not alone among modern philosophers in proposing simple proofs for the existence of God that could not be denied. Of course there was Pascal as well, looking warily on, preferring the God of Abraham and Isaac to the God of the philosophers. If subjectivity was to provide the base, Pascal preferred the subjectivity of faith. But by and large philosophers adopted the epistemological turn taken by Descartes and saw as their first task to establish that their ideas had non-mental counterparts. From Descartes through Hegel, philosophers took it to be a necessity to establish God's existence if they were to know anything

---

3. The traditional sequence from world to man to God has become the sequence from man to God to world.

else and they did so to their satisfaction. With exceptions of course. But there was a remarkable persistence of the notion that subjectivity, that is, the knowing subject, comes thematically first.

Perhaps no one has seen more acutely than Cornelio Fabro that atheism was already latent in the Cartesian turn. *Incipit tragoedia hominis moderni!* Fabro regards modern thought, as characterized by the Cartesian turn, to be essentially atheistic. Despite the more or less explicit profession of theism on the part of the majority of modern philosophers through the nineteenth century, "this remains largely in the realm of good intentions and reveals the personal commitment of individual philosophers," which will inevitably run afoul of their principles.[4]

Descartes considered it the task of philosophy, rather than theology, to handle the questions of God and the soul. Kant sought to battle atheism and incredulity. Bacon thought that sips of philosophy might conduce to atheism, but full drafts aid religion. Leibniz too, of course, and, again, Hegel, who takes us well into the nineteenth century. But Fabro puts before us contemporaries of such philosophers who saw more clearly than they the logical outcome of their starting-point. If Fabro is right, it would be unwise for a theist to take the Cartesian turn as good money and seek to do business within that assumption. This is Fabro's point, and of course it was Kierkegaard's too. (It is no accident that Fabro, one of the preeminent Thomists of his time, was the principal translator of Kierkegaard into Italian.)

You and I have been raised in a philosophical atmosphere that has drawn the atheistic consequences of the subjective or epistemological turn. We may almost feel nostalgia for the problem Kierkegaard faced. Of course we theists today face very similar problems among ourselves. But the dominant view has been inhospitable to natural theology.

The philosophical ambiance of the century that is drawing to a close, at least in English-speaking philosophy, arose from the perceived collapse of the epistemological project. What came to be called Representationalism was seen to have insurmountable difficulties attached to it. But the first revolt was against the Idealism that was the last gasp of the epistemological turn. The worry about how Thought related to Being ended with the identification of the two: Thought and Being are one. No problem. No wonder empiricism was just around the corner.

---

4. See Cornelio Fabro, *Introduzione all'Ateismo Moderno* (Rome: Editrice Studium, 1964), 77.

If the principal problem of philosophy was to determine which of our ideas and judgments matched something outside the mind—what is in the mind being taken as primary—it turned out to be very difficult to restore a world that had been put into the epistemological dock. Increasingly, the contribution our minds make to the object of knowledge took center stage. Things in themselves are, after all, designated as 'sensible' and 'intelligible' things, denominated from the fact that they can be known. But to be intelligible or sensible, from being an extrinsic denomination, became constitutive of the objects of sense and intellect.

Prior to the modern turn, the contribution our mind makes in our knowing of things had been discussed under two rubrics: the relation of the concept to what was conceived, and the relation of more or less vague cognitive contents to one another and to singular existents. Aristotelians had arranged our grasp of substance on a Porphyrean tree of greater or lesser generality. I can think of a mouse as a thing, as alive, as a wee beastie, or as Mickey. Generic and specific and finally individual grasps of the thing. But how do substance and animate and mouse relate to Mickey or to one another? Is Mickey Mouse just another thing in a world where substance as such and animal as such and mouse as such can also be found? The Problem of Universals, stated by Porphyry in his Introduction to Aristotle's *Categories*, consisted of three intercepting questions. Are genera and species real or imaginary? If real, are they material or immaterial? If immaterial, do they exist apart from material things or somehow with them?

Having posed the problem, Porphyry pronounced it too difficult to discuss then and there, and went on to discuss genus, species, difference, property, and accident, leaving their ontological status up in the air. During the early Middle Ages particularly, when texts conveying ancient philosophical thought were rare, this work of Porphyry was commented on again and again. And what commentator could resist the lure of a problem too difficult to take up now? No one shared Porphyry's diffidence, and commentaries on his Isagoge all attempt a solution of the problem. The most satisfying resolution of it, perhaps most clearly stated by Thomas Aquinas,[5] is that, since our minds naturally

---

5. Already in the youthful *De ente et essentia*, Thomas distinguishes clearly between the nature as such (*natura absolute considerata*) and what may incidentally attach to that nature: in the mind, logical relations; in matter, individuation. Thus, genus and species are incidental, not constitutive features, of the nature.

move from the vague to the specific, the different readings of an object do not add to the inventory of the real world. As it progresses toward more specific knowledge of a thing, the mind relates its different grasps to one another and to the individual. A genus, Porphyry said, is something said of many specifically different things. A species is something said of many numerically different things. Animal is a more general grasp of Mickey than is mouse. Animal is a genus. A mouse is a species. But to be a genus is to be said of many things. Is that what we mean by animal? An animal is a living being endowed with sensation. How to compare that definition and the fact that animal is a genus? To be predicated or to be more or less general is not part of the definition of animal. For it to be predicated, for it to be conceived, is not what an animal is. What an animal is, the cognitive content, is neither singular nor universal. Universals—genus, species, et al.—are relations the mind attaches to things in knowing them and are not features of the world as such.

One could go on of course. But my point is the simple one that in pre-modern discussions of knowing reality the contribution of the mind was not ignored. But this contribution did not swamp the object known. After the epistemological turn, our mind's contribution becomes increasingly dominant and defining of reality. Substance, cause, effect—these are the grooves of our mind, the way we are fated or fashioned to think of things. But what of things as they are independently of our thinking of them? After such a question, a silence grows. What would it be like to know things when we do not know them? Noumena recede to the very edges of the mind, and with Hegel disappear. Things are *as they are known* and there is nothing more to be said.

The linguistic turn was taken by those who did not ask whether the assumptions of the epistemological turn were faulty. All references to mental activity in the old sense were set aside and attention focused on language. If knowledge as mental representation of the real ran into so many difficulties, it was attractive to think that there was an immediate relation of language to things. Bertrand Russell, fresh from the achievement of the *Principia Mathematica,* thought that the grammar of mathematical logic could accommodate an empirical vocabulary with the result that the establishment of the truth or falsity of non-tautological propositions would be a relatively easy matter. Molecular propositions are true or false depending on the truth or falsity of their constitutive atomic propositions which are ultimate. φx is the form of an atomic proposition and Russell, at least, thought that the elements of such a proposition could be put into one-to-one relation with the elements of the corresponding physical state of affairs.

It was of course fatal that the verification of atomic propositions was so explained. This paved the way for Logical Positivism and the bumptious dogmatism of the youthful A. J. Ayer in his 1936 book, *Language, Truth and Logic*. Meaningful propositions are either tautologies or empirical propositions, Ayer breezily assured his readers. The former are true thanks to their logical form, the latter are true or false with reference to empirical facts. Ayer's book is unmistakably a young man's book. Descartes may have begun with doubt, but Ayer seems never to have had one. His book had the verve and sweep that made it a favorite of beginners in philosophy. With respect to God and morality, Ayer's message was straightforward. Since neither of these alleged disciplines is made up of either tautologies or empirical propositions, they consist, not of falsehoods, but of nonsense. The Principle of Verifiability was the Procrustean bed on which pretentious limbs were merrily lopped off the body of knowledge.

This is the philosophical atmosphere in which my generation grew up. Wittgenstein's *Tractatus* was usually read, rightly or wrongly, as a crisper statement of Russell's logical atomism. Although news of this was slow to reach many philosophers, Logical Positivism was quickly consigned to the dust bin of history, and for two reasons. First, it was hoist on its own petard. The Principle of Meaning was this: a proposition is meaningful if and only if it is either a tautology or an empirical generalization. Is the principle itself meaningful? Since it is neither a tautology nor an empirical generalization, it could only survive as prescriptive, that is, as an arbitrary decision as to what one would consider meaningful. The second reason derived from the posthumously published works of Wittgenstein.

One of the abiding effects of logical empiricism was its assumption that natural language was in bad shape, a jumble of equivocations, difficult to interpret. Thus in manuals of formal logic, the discipline about to be studied was commended because its formalism enabled the student to rise above the ambiguities of natural language to the pure univocity of symbols. In this heady atmosphere, which the previous study of mathematics made congenial to many students, there was no need to ask what one was talking about. One was merely minding his p's and q's and r's. It was the relations between these symbols, variables which took sentences for their arguments, that was pursued. But in introductions to beginning texts the promise was held out that, equipped with this formal logic, one could descend into the ambiguity of ordinary language and introduce some semblance of order there. The great assumption was that ordinary language was a misleading mess and no one could begin to figure it out until he studied logic. But surely this was merely to put off the evil day. The application of formal logic to ordinary language required that the symbols be interpreted in terms of a natural as opposed to an artificial language. But natural language is hopelessly muddled. There must be some way of unmuddling it before applying to it the symbols of formal logic.

I like to imagine Wittgenstein riding a bus and suddenly beginning to eavesdrop on the conversations going on around him. Everyone is talking a mile a minute and no one seems incapable of following his interlocutor. Wittgenstein has an epiphany. Nothing is wrong with ordinary language! It is a remarkably supple and sophisticated instrument that just about everybody has already mastered. Speakers were not awaiting the ministrations of formal logic in order to speak successfully, that is, minimally, to mean something. This epiphany could have been followed by another: introductory formal logic texts are written in more or less ordinary English, presumed already known by the reader and an intelligible enough medium in which to teach logic.

Logical Empiricism was an extension of the assumption of how logic applies to the world. Ordinary language had either to be verifiable with reference to empirical facts or be judged meaningless. To the degree that language could be parsed into the patois of empirical generalizations it might be thought meaningful. The assumption was that the basic language, the controlling use of language, is empirical science—which uses as little language as it can.

Wittgenstein's imagined bus-born epiphany—it is the bus, not the epiphany that is imagined—led him to dismiss that. All kinds of language-uses are perfectly in order as they are, without any need to reduce them to some supposedly regulative language game, that of empirical generalizations. During the heyday of Logical Empiricism there were misguided theists who sought to re-express their beliefs in terms of "verifiable propositions." One could read in *Mind* an article explaining that "God is love" can be translated into "We have the sense that we are loved." The most obvious beneficiary of Wittgenstein's notion of a plurality of okay language games was religious language. Once under Positivist embargo, along with moral language, religious language was now said to be in order just as it was. It had its own internal rules, not just anything could be said, but its meaningfulness was not conditional on its being translated into empirical generalizations. Religious language thus looked self-justifying. The sigh of relief from theists and religious believers blew craft back and forth across the Atlantic. Once again it was possible to speak of God in respectable philosophical circles.

It was not long before this gift horse was looked in the mouth. Actually, it was Kai Nielsen, a Canadian atheist, doubtless annoyed by all those grinning theists, who described the new dispensation as Wittgensteinian Fideism. Now, Fideism is not a word often used to flatter. It is in fact a heresy condemned by the Church. What Nielsen perceived was that the reconciliation of theism and Wittgensteinian language theory was effectively the abandonment of natural theology or any need to show that it was reasonable to talk about God. That this had lately been taken to mean the translatability of religious language into atomic propositions, or else, was one thing. But to dismiss all efforts to justify it had its problems. The religious language game is played. But by whom? How does one become involved in it? By birth and upbringing, perhaps by membership in a given society or culture? Most Christians are baptized into it and at home and school, in church, they learn the knack of religious language.

But how does one get into it by choice and design? Is learning a religious language like learning English as a foreign language? Or can one go to Berlitz and take lessons? Is speaking the language to make truth claims? What goes on when one abandons the language? And so forth and so on and on.

THE LATEST ADIEU TO PHILOSOPHY

Philosophy in our century has been both hostile and friendly to theism and the project of natural theology. Believers sought accommodations in either case. There were those—many of them theologians—who thought the transcendence of God, let alone the mysteries of the faith, had to be jettisoned in order to accommodate the "modern mind" as represented by Logical Empiricism.[6] There seemed to be a necessary connection between electricity and the Enlightenment. On the other hand, there were many who welcomed the notion that religion is a self-contained language game that need not establish its bona fides by reduction to the language game of natural science.

Such swift accounts as I have attempted suggest that philosophy is a kind of reptile that abandons one skin after another. It can certainly seem that, since Descartes, the philosophical undertaking has been largely a matter of burying one's predecessors. Part of the excitement of reading Descartes, when young, is discovering that whole centuries of thought about which one knows nothing were wholly wrongheaded. It is exhilarating to achieve even a borrowed condescension in one fell swoop. That Descartes himself was relatively young, just out of college, when he saw through the pretenses of all previous centuries, adds to the excitement. The same surge of excitement was available to the young in reading Ayer's 1936 book. With Descartes, as far later with Ayer, such negative dismissals are meant to clear the path for the positive. Descartes flattered himself that he had not only reduced all previous philosophy to rubble, he had also and more importantly put the quest for truth on a sure course such that the future would be an extended footnote to what he had begun.

This was not to be. It was the iconoclasm of Descartes that proved more contagious than his positive teaching. Modern philosophy became an Oedipal tradition of destroying one's intellectual fathers. Once thinkers had described themselves as standing on the shoulders of the giants who preceded them. Now they had a foot firmly planted on the neck of their fallen fathers. Sometimes it was an earlier version of the philosopher himself that had to be exorcised—Kant made the great turn from pre-critical into critical philosophy. In our days Heidegger and Wittgenstein undertook mid-course corrections that distanced them from their early work.

---

6. On the continent, theologians like Rudolph Bultmann accepted the equivalent of Logical Empiricism. Bultmann's demythologizing of religion "begins with the premise that no one who uses electricity and listens to the radio can any longer believe in the miracle world of the New Testament." (See the Gifford Lectures of E. L. Mascall, *The Openness of Being* [Philadelphia: Westminster Press, 1971], 206.)

Natural theology now confronts a challenge more disarming than any previous one. The epistemological turn ushered in a succession of attempts to relate mind to matter, thought to reality. The linguistic turn is taken when thought as representation is set aside and efforts are made to put language into relation with the world without the intermediary of mind. The sheer suppleness and surprise of actual language led on to talk of language games. What has lately happened can be thought of as a twist in the linguistic turn or the sharpest curve yet taken in modern philosophy.

If for centuries philosophy had been a series of efforts to rid itself of its past, this was done in order to enable the thing finally to be done in a way that was not open to criticism. With the linguistic turn, alliances between continental and English-speaking philosophers became possible. Finally it was recognized that the task of philosophy is to show that philosophy itself is the problem. *The task of philosophy as traditionally understood, despite the Sicilian Vespers that characterized its recent history, was not something that could be done well as opposed to badly.* It cannot be done at all. It is mistaken through and through. If only one could say that.

Why not? I just did. The problem is that this enormously important insight cannot be said in such a way that the statement expressing it is true.

A little book of John-Paul Sartre, published shortly after the end of World War II, like the little book of Ayer already referred to, provided a popular account of the vertigo the mind must feel after having cast off all previous efforts to know the truth. *Existentialism Is a Humanism* drew out the implications of the atheism that had become the assumption of most philosophers. It could be described as Nietzsche Lite.

Both Plato and Aristotle and generations of thinkers who followed them assumed that it is our destiny to know the nature of things. Philosophical theism in its various forms is the recognition that the world around us needs an eternal and necessary cause. Sartre chides those who think that God can be removed from this picture and everything else remain the same. The denial of God, Sartre insists—and he himself was an atheist—changes everything radically. The theist holds that God is to the world as the maker is to the artifact. The artisan realizes an idea; so too, the created thing embodies a purpose that is its nature. As creatures, human beings have a nature which provides the clue as to what they ought to do and become, a measure by which they can be said to be flourishing or not. Sartre summarizes this in the slogan: *essence precedes existence.* By existence here he means human existence, that is, behavior, moral action. If God exists, things are required of us. To take God out of the picture brings about its total collapse. Man no longer has a nature. There are no guidelines prior to acting as to what is good and what is bad. Human agents no longer make choices with reference to independent criteria of right and wrong. Now they must will the criteria in virtue of which they choose. *Existence precedes essence.*

Compared with Sartre's essay, A. J. Ayer's book seems almost addled in the cheerful way in which it waves away all language other than empirical reports. It is as if, that done, one can go on living as before, relying on one's banker, leaving a bicycle unguarded, trusting one's spouse. Perhaps it is just a matter of style and only Sartre saw the need to feel gloomy about it. For all I know A. J. Ayer lay shivering in his bed at night, terrified by the realization that good and bad were merely expressions of the way he feels. And at that moment he was feeling very bad indeed.

The linguistic turn has in recent years taken on a decidedly German accent. The vatic ruminations of Heidegger have been crossed with the epigrammatic suggestiveness of the later Wittgenstein. It is now taken for granted by many that the traditional aspirations of philosophy have to be abandoned. The absence of God, it has been realized, entails the absence of the world as well. There is no there there of which our knowledge could be the true expression. Mental activity is no longer the grasp of the real, there being no real to grasp. So what are we speaking of?

Language is no longer the sign of thought and thought is no longer the grasp of nature, of essence, of the way things are. We are thrown back on language itself, and to language is assigned the great task of constructing the self we are and the world in which we live. Language is a set of rules we adopt for purely pragmatic or utilitarian reasons. We no longer seek to achieve the true and avoid the false. Forget about both of those. The only question is, does it work, is it successful.

But that of course only puts off the evil day. When we ask ourselves what is the end or purpose of that which works, or what is the use it is meant to serve, we are once more thrown back on ourselves. Our purposes are not given in the nature of things. Whatever I say is sayable because it is permitted by the rules of the language we speak. I cannot talk of something beyond or outside of language. Whatever I say is inescapably within language itself. This has strange consequences. As Lescek Kolokowski put it:

> In other words, I have to obey a rule ordering me to keep in mind that whatever I am saying I am not saying that something is the case—nothing being the case—the rules give me the right to say so: this amounts to stating that we all are to speak only in a kind of metalanguage.[7]

Talk is really only about talking—only it turns out that we really cannot say that.

Once atheist philosophers were wont to say that they rejected theism because it is false. On the basis of the philosophical attitude just sketched, it is no longer possible to say that. The philosophical attitude itself cannot be described as true or correct. Theism thus is no worse off, and no better off, than anything else.

Cold comfort, of course.

Some years ago, Michael Foster wrote an essay called "'We' in Modern Philosophy." I have only vague memories of its content—sometimes we remember little more than good titles—but I do remember that he was addressing the way in which philosophical claims were regularly presented in the first person plural. Philosophers had a way of speaking for the race rather than themselves. This was, and doubtless was intended to be, intimidating. How as a member of the race could one take exception to what the race is saying?

This tendency has grown more prevalent since Foster wrote. Reclusive or antic thinkers, the bashful and the brazen both, regularly speak what is on the mind of modern man. The history of modern philosophy since Descartes becomes increasingly a history of received opinions—received and then rejected. One is told what everyone prior to Descartes did. One is told what everyone did up until the linguistic turn. One is told of the way we think now.

Despite the accommodations that some theists have made to one passing form of philosophy or another, it is increasingly clear that

7. Lescek Kolokowski, *Metaphysical Horror* (Oxford: Basil Blackwell, 1988), 4.

theism presupposes a pretty thorough rejection of what has been going on in philosophy in the last third of the second millennium. As Fabro has argued—and Thomas Reid says something similar with respect to the abandonment of common sense—something begins with Descartes that has atheism as its logical consequence. That consequence has now been drawn. It should be obvious that theists would be unwise to seek to state their case in terms of philosophies that are essentially atheistic. But theologians, alas, irrepressibly attempt this, as witness their odd fondness for Heidegger.

Kierkegaard's Johannes Climacus saw what modern philosophy was doing to theism and Christian belief. He undertook to refute modern philosophy root and branch. Whatever one makes of his effort, and its assumptions, surely he had the right aim. The possibility of natural theology can only be seen when one has called into question the assumptions of the turn philosophy made with Descartes. Subsequent turns presuppose the first. And they have brought us to nihilism.

Us? We? In my next lecture I shall call attention to a more or less unbroken philosophical tradition that runs like a subterranean river through the centuries of the modern hegemony and is now emerging to the attention of those who realize they do not wish to be included in the "we" of modern philosophy.

OCTOBER 28, 1999

Atheism Is Not the Default Position

Nam atheismus, integre consideratus, non est quid originarium.

Gaudium et spes, n. 19

LUCTUS ET ANGOR

The day before Vatican II (the ecumenical council held from 1962 to 1965) ceremoniously ended, a document called the Pastoral Constitution on the Church in the Modern World was promulgated by Paul VI. It is by far the longest of the sixteen documents of that council. In the custom which dates from before the age of printing, the document is known by its *incipit* or opening words, as well as by its descriptive title. *Gaudium et spes*. Joy and Hope. Those words might suggest that the Church's survey of the world in which it must work was sunny and optimistic. But this is as misleading as it would be if the document were known by the next two words in the opening sentence, *luctus et angor*. *"The joy and hope, the grief and anguish, of men of the present time, especially of the poor and afflicted, must be the joy and hope, grief and anguish of Christ's disciples as well, since there is nothing truly human that can fail to resonate in their hearts"* (n. 1). There follows a remarkable look at the modern world which, despite the changes of the intervening thirty-five years, remains of interest.

Human beings seek answers to the ever recurring questions people ask about the meaning of the present life and of the life to come. But if we are defined by the need to ask such questions, this has been obscured by various features of modern culture. The rise of atheism is seen as the negation of the dignity of the human person because that dignity consists in a call to live happily with his creator forever.

> Human dignity rests above all on the fact that man is called to communion with God. This invitation to converse with God is issued to a man as soon as he is born, for he only exists because God has created him with love and through love continues to keep him in existence. He cannot live fully in the truth unless he freely acknowledges that love and entrusts himself to his creator.[1]

Hence the rather extended anatomy of atheism that follows, eight forms of which are distinguished. There are those who expressly deny God; there are others who say that no assertion can be made about him, perhaps because they adopt restrictive methods which have precisely that result. For example, by holding that everything must be expressed in the language of science. Others deny the existence of absolute truth. Yet others think that the affirmation of man entails the denial of God. Sometimes God is rejected because of a faulty notion of what he is. Some seem indifferent to the question, others are prompted by the evil in the world. Finally, the world is too much with us and our minds never lift above the particular task to the meaning of it all.

That an ecumenical council of the Catholic Church should name atheism as the bane of the modern world will not come as a complete surprise to anyone. But in what professes to be a realistic look at the world to which she hopes to minister, the Church speaks of atheism as by and large an achieved or acquired position. It is not the natural state of the human mind, but the loss of something.

---

1. *Gaudium et spes*, n. 19. The translation is my own. Surely it is a sign of the times that these noble documents are now made available in "a completely revised translation in inclusive language." The resultant bad English is a source of laughter and tears, *gaudium et luctus*. Inclusive English excludes the great monuments of the language but perhaps teams of right-thinking mistranslators will do to the Western Canon what they have already done to Scripture and liturgical documents.

There are of course counterexamples to any generalization about human beings, and there are instances in which we are assured that a person simply had no thought about God at all, one way or the other. A notable instance of this is André Frossard. (See his *Dieu existe, je l'ai recontré* [Paris: Fayard, 1970].) He tells us that, although his father was the first general secretary of the French communist party, there was no talk at all about God in his home, nor did the environs prompt such thoughts in him. He is looking back on a past that seems astounding to him from the vantage point of a convert. His conversion was without prelude. He stepped into a church a non-theist, a non-believer, with no intention other than whiling away some time until a friend arrived. He emerged some minutes later a confirmed believer. Many expressed skepticism about the elements of this account. Frossard is narrating it many years after it happened. On what basis do we correct another's experience, or memory of his experience? But by and large, speaking of modern atheism, it does seem to be true that people usually become atheists by losing their childhood beliefs. The original position was belief, theism, and then, as the alpha privative suggests, it was lost and the result was atheism.

Vatican II was not the first time that the Church had addressed the modern world nor the first time it had sought to characterize that world. In 1878, a frail old man had been elected pope to succeed Pius IX whose phenomenally long reign prompted the electors to guard against another long papacy by electing Cardinal Pecci, already advanced in age. He took the name Leo XIII and he would be pope for a quarter century. Like his predecessor he took a dim view of the modern world, and he thought that there were things that ought to be done about it. In an encyclical letter called *Aeterni Patris*,[2] he proposed as a remedy to the intellectual and social evils of the time a return to the thought of Thomas Aquinas.

There is something poignant about this. It was under Pius IX that the papal states were lost to the new political forces in Italy. Pius had literally been chased from the Vatican and when he returned to the Vatican from Gaieta, humbled and beaten by the forces against which he had warned, he never left again. Leo XIII was the first elected "prisoner

---

2. Its *incipit*; its actual title was *On Restoring in Catholic Schools Christian Philosophy according to the Mind of St Thomas Aquinas the Angelic Doctor.*

of the Vatican," living out his reign as pope in the diminutive sovereign state that was the almost risible contradictory of his spiritual hegemony. Neutral observers might be astonished by the spectacle of the representative of a Church diagnosing the ills of the modern world and proposing the study of a thirteenth-century Dominican as the way out of impending disaster. The *kulturkampf* was well under way in Bismarck's Germany. France was scarcely better off, although it called its condition progress. Modernity did not consider itself in need of remedy and it seemed in the ascendancy everywhere.

One observer, the Gifford lecturer in Aberdeen just a century ago, Josiah Royce wrote an appraisal of Leo's philosophical movement that was anything but negative.[3] Royce was a star of the American philosophical establishment and not given to antic thinking. True, he had published a novel,[4] but then so had George Santayana. There is an almost total absence in Royce's appraisal of *Aeterni Patris* of the fact that it was meant to address a crisis in modern thought. Apart from the undeniable merits of Aquinas, Royce saw the encyclical as licensing Catholic thinkers to enter the mainstream of modern philosophy. Furthermore, he foretold what would be called Modernism, the adoption by Catholic thinkers of positions of dubious compatibility with their ostensible beliefs with the consequent redefinition of what Christianity is. The influence of Kant on Catholic thinkers is noted and applauded. All in all, Royce's essay exudes satisfaction with the current condition of philosophy. He betrays none of the melancholy Matthew Arnold expressed so memorably in 1867.

> The Sea of Faith
> Was once, too, at the full, and round earth's shore
> Lay like the folds of a bright girdle furl'd.
> But now I only hear

---

3. "Pope Leo's Philosophical Movement and Its Relations to Modern Thought" appeared first in the Boston *Evening Transcript* on July 29, 1903 and was reprinted in *Fugitive Essays by Josiah Royce,* with an introduction by Dr. J. Loewenberg (Cambridge, Mass.: Harvard University Press, 1925), 408–429.

4. Josiah Royce, *The Feud of Oakfield Creek, a Novel of California Life* (New York and London: Johnson Reprint, 1970). The novel was originally published in 1887 in a print run of 1,500 copies. Demand, it was said, never outran supply. Santayana, Royce's colleague, mentions Royce's disappointment at the abrupt ending of his career as a novelist.

Its melancholy, long, withdrawing roar,
Retreating, to the breath
Of the night-wind, down the vast edges drear
And naked shingles of the world.

In such prose works as *God and the Bible* and *Literature and Dogma* Arnold is the champion of the cultural changes of the time, but in *Dover Beach* there is no gloating about the receding influence of belief in God. What comes through is rather a romantic despair.

Ah, love, let us be true
To one another! For the world, which seems
To lie before us like a land of dreams,
So various, so beautiful, so new,
Hath really neither joy, nor love, nor light,
Nor certitude, nor peace, nor help for pain;
And we are here as on a darkling plain
Swept with confused alarms of struggle and flight,
Where ignorant armies clash by night.

That is much more like the world of Pius IX and Leo.[5] Nonetheless, Arnold far more explicitly than Royce held that Christianity would have to be fundamentally rethought in the light of modern knowledge. The difference is that Arnold was depressed by the loss.

Is it fanciful to see in Leo's apprehension about the direction the modern world had taken an anticipation of the negative assessments of modernity and the Enlightenment which have characterized the last quarter of the twentieth century? Lescek Kolokowski suggests just that. "It appears as if we suddenly woke up to perceive things which the humble, and not necessarily highly educated, priests have been seeing— and warning about—for three centuries and which they have repeatedly denounced in their Sunday sermons. They kept telling their flocks that a world that has forgotten God has forgotten the very distinction

---

5. Writing to his mother in June 1869, Arnold said, "My poems represent, on the whole, the main movement of mind in the last quarter of a century, and thus they will probably have their day as people become conscious to themselves of what that movement of mind is." (See Introduction, *Matthew Arnold, Prose and Poetry*, ed. Archibald L. Bouton, The Modern Student's Library [New York: Charles Scribner's Sons, 1927], xv).

between good and evil and has made life meaningless, sunk into ni-hilism."[6] Well, Leo was highly educated as is his present successor John Paul II who in 1998 issued a small book of an encyclical called *Fides et ratio* which was meant to give new life to the movement inaugurated by Leo XIII.

Having begun in the middle, let us turn now to the beginning of modern philosophy. That René Descartes did not see the turn he had taken as conducive to atheism, indeed quite the reverse, is clear from the mystical experience that inspired the path he took.

Two Memorials

René Descartes died in Stockholm in 1650 where he had gone to tutor the brilliant young queen Christina. There was found among his effects a written account of a dream which had been the genesis of his great innovative efforts as a philosopher.[7] The great event took place in 1619 when Descartes was twenty-three and in winter quarters at Ulm. The dream involved three stages between which Descartes awoke, or dreamed that he did. In the first, he is back at LaFlèche, the Jesuit college he had attended, and he is trying to get to the college chapel to pray, fighting against a wind which slams him against the wall of the church when he turns to look after someone he had passed without greeting. Then in the court of the college he is told that someone he knows has left him a melon. He awakes depressed. Fallen asleep again, he is awakened by a clap of thunder to find sparks of fire filling his room. In the third dream he sees on a table two books, a dictionary and a *Corpus poetarum*, opened on a verse of Ausonius: *quod vitae sectabor iter: what path of life should I take?* Then he is given a slip on which *Est* and *Non* (*yes* and *no*) are written. Descartes himself subjected this dream to close analysis. The dictionary represents the totality of science, the anthology

---

6. See his *Modernity on Endless Trial* (Chicago: University of Chicago Press, 1990).

7. The best discussion of this once neglected dream is Jacques Maritain's *Le songe de Descartes*, in *Oeuvres complètes*, ed. Rene Mougel et al., vol. 5 (Paris: Editions Saint-Paul, 1982), 13–222. The earlier treatment of Descartes in *Three Reformers* (ibid., vol. 3, 485–521) is an ingenious likening of Descartes's account of human knowledge to Thomas Aquinas's account of the knowledge of the angels.

of poets the marriage of philosophy and wisdom. Yes and No represent truth and falsity in profane science, the quotation from Ausonius is the good advice of someone wise, perhaps Moral Theology personified. The wind is an evil spirit that seeks to prevent him from getting to the chapel. In the morning, a grateful Descartes vowed to make a pilgrimage to Loretto in thanksgiving to the Blessed Virgin, a vow he fulfilled five years later.

All our knowledge of this event, the dreams, their interpretation, are at secondhand. The account that Descartes had made as a constant reminder to himself was read and commented on by others after his death, but it has not come down to us. Leibniz copied portions of it, others mention it. The pious chronicler of Descartes's life—his account of Descartes's death is graphic and moving—invites us to a quite different understanding of the Father of Modern Philosophy than is common. In Stockholm Descartes has a spiritual advisor, he confesses and receives the Eucharist just before he falls ill, he is given the last rites and dies with the priest at his bedside. Descartes set out to reform science, but the Reformation, through whose first phase he was living—he spent much of his life in Protestant countries—seems not to have affected his faith.

But it is the fact that Descartes begins the revolution in philosophy under religious auspices, convinced that, among other things, he can offer a proof of God's existence, that sets his off from the far more famous Memorial of his near contemporary Blaise Pascal.

It was four years after the death of Descartes, on another November night, the 23rd, "feast of Saint Clement, pope and martyr, and of others in the Martyrology, eve of the feast of St. Chrysogonus, martyr," that an event took place that bridged the two days, beginning at 10:30 on the 23rd and continuing until 12:30 of the 24th. What occurred was so pivotal for Pascal that he wrote it down. A few days after his death in 1662, a servant found sewn into his coat a piece of parchment, carefully folded to contain a sheet of paper. On the paper was an apparently contemporary note, made soon after the experience, which is copied with changes onto the parchment, indicating that Pascal carried on his person not one but two reminders of the event he doubtless would have remembered without them. This Memorial was transferred from coat to coat, from lining to lining, sewn in each time, during the years from the

"Night of Fire" until Pascal's death. For eight years after the great event, Pascal had this reminder constantly with him.[8]

What does the Memorial contain? He who runs as he reads will find the contents of the Memorial disjointed and confused. Perhaps they triggered off the memory of the writer, but the experience can scarcely be conveyed by a few words. After the careful notation of the day, already quoted, Pascal writes in the center of the page FIRE. And then, "God of Abraham, God of Isaac, God of Jacob, not of the philosophers and savants. Certitude, certitude, feeling, joy, peace. The God of Jesus Christ." And so on.

Scholars have shown that the composition of the Memorial is careful, not just random jottings.[9] For one thing, the distinction between the God of the philosophers and the God of Abraham is not just a verbal contrast: the Memorial is a florilegium of biblical texts and allusions. The contrast with Descartes's dream could not be more fundamental. Descartes awoke with the sense that his intellectual mission had divine sanction; Pascal recovered from his great experience convinced that the God of the philosophers must be held at bay and the God of the Bible, the God of Jesus Christ, receive complete attention.

Faith and Reason

There is another lesson to be drawn from considering these deeply felt and decisive mystical experiences of two figures who stand at the divide between modern philosophy and what had gone before. The two were devout Catholics. Their religious faith was the ambiance within which they pursued their intellectual work. Both were mathematicians, of course, a discipline that might seem quite remote from questions about the ultimate destiny of human beings, but one's convictions about human destiny and ultimate reality form the human envelope within which even mathematics is engaged.

8. First published in 1740, the Memorial is usually included in editions of the *Pensees*. I am consulting the text as it is found in *Oeuvres complètes*, preface de Henri Gouhier, presentation et notes de Louis LaFuma (Paris: Editions du Seuil, 1963), 618.

9. See Marvin O'Connell, *Blaise Pascal, Reasons of the Heart* (Grand Rapids, Mich.: Eerdmans, 1997), Chapter 5 "The Night of Fire," 90–103.

As believers, Descartes and Pascal represent one of the divisions that has been present from the earliest centuries of Christianity. Indeed there is biblical warrant for Pascal's attitude as well as Descartes. *Videte ne quis vos decipiat per philosophiam*, St. Paul warns the Colossians, "Beware lest you be led astray by philosophy," but that same Paul, in Acts, speaks to the Athenians of the God they had come to know by rational means, and announces that this God became man in Jesus.

Paul here and in Romans 1:19 assumes that human beings can come to know that God exists. This knowledge then must be related to the mysteries of the faith, what God has told us of himself. For some believers, the existence of God was all but self-evident. It is not unimportant that Descartes, in his dedication of his *Meditations métaphysiques* to the theologians of the Sorbonne, quotes these very texts. How do the attitudes of Pascal and Descartes to their faith differ from that which characterized the Scholastic tradition it was Descartes's intention to replace?

THE PRIOR IN HIS CHOIR STALL

About a thousand years ago, in a monastery at Bec in Normandy, the prior occupied the first stall on the left when the monks gathered for mass and to chant the office. The office or function of the monks was the *opus Dei* and in the context God's work entailed singing the entire psalter of David once a week, with some psalms sung several times in the course of the week. The days of the week in turn were measured by the canonical hours—Matins, Lauds, Prime, Terce, Sext, None, Vespers, Compline—the times at which the monks gathered to chant a selection of psalms, listen to readings from other parts of Scripture, and lift their voices in the appropriate hour's hymn. This went on from the early hours of morning, through the day, at three-hour intervals, to the twilight hour of Vespers and finally Compline, at which the Song of Simeon—*Nunc dimittis servum tuum Domine, secundum verbum tuum in pace*—would send the monks to their beds.

The prior's name was Anselm. Eventually, like his predecessor as prior, Lanfranc, he would become Archbishop of Canterbury, but he did not of course know that as he lived those long years in the monastery trying to bring his life into conformity with the evangelical counsels. When he first arrived in Normandy, he had been the prize student of Lanfranc. Eventually, Anselm was given the role of teacher. From his pen during these years came a number of writings, most of them relatively short, many of them cast in the form of dialogues, which still interest those involved in their subjects. *On truth. On the fall of the devil. On the grammarian.* Medievalists still pore over these, but there are other writings of Prior Anselm that nearly all philosophers have read and on which all have settled views. They concern the mind's ability to know that God exists.

A rejected title for one of them, derivative from Augustine, has had a career of its own: *Fides quaerens intellectum*, faith seeking understanding. In the event, Anselm gave them Greek titles, *Proslogion* and *Monologion*. It is the *Proslogion* that interests us here. We can imagine Anselm getting the inspiration for its argument while in choir, when Psalm 41 was being chanted. The very familiarity of the psalm had perhaps hidden from him the import of its opening line. *Dixit insipiens in corde suo, non est Deus: The fool has said in his heart, there is no God.* Suddenly it dawned on Anselm that the denial of God is foolish because it cannot really be done. If you know what the word means, you are unable to say that God does not exist. Of course Anselm spelled it out, availing himself of verses from other psalms as he proceeded.

"God" means that than which nothing greater can be thought.

Anselm then ponders the meaning of "greater" and suggests that if we consider the relation of an artisan to his work, we can say that before he begins he has in mind what he will do and when he is done he has effected it in wood or stone or whatever. Very well. To exist in the mind is one thing, to exist in the external world another. The table existing in the mind of the artisan can be assigned the value of 1. The table existing outside the mind also gets a value of 1. Then, when the idea has been realized and exists both in the mind and outside the mind, the result is greater, viz. $1 + 1 = 2$. With this elementary observation in hand, Anselm can show why the denial of God's existence is impossible, foolish, incoherent.

1.   If to be in the mind and to be in reality is greater than to be in the mind alone,
2.   And if anyone who understands the word "God" has God in mind,
3.   And what he has in mind is the idea of something than which nothing greater can be thought,

4. Then if one denies that God exists, that is, denies that he exists out-side the mind, he is saying that there is something greater than that than which nothing greater can be thought—namely the thought that God is both in the mind and in reality. God in the mind = 1; God outside the mind = 1. The combination of these is greater than the first alone. To deny the combination is in conflict with the agreed upon meaning of "God."

5. So it is foolish to say, in the heart or out loud, that God does not exist. It is self-contradictory.

This is to make knowledge of God's existence *quid originarium* in-deed, it and not atheism is the default position of the human mind. Fur-thermore, in defending the claim by reducing to absurdity its contra-dictory, Anselm suggests that "God exists" is self-evident to the human mind.[10] Under the influence of Karl Barth, it has become fashionable to suggest that Anselm's proof was meant to be effective only within the ambience of Christian faith. That is, he begins holding that there is a God and he ends holding that there is a God, but this conviction does not repose on the proof he has offered. It is a matter of faith seeking un-derstanding, but the understanding does not provide an underpinning for the faith: it presupposes it. It can of course be wondered whether Anselm had ever met an atheist. Presumably there were none within the walls of the monastery, and his secular experience prior to entering would not seem to have brought him into atheistic circles, if there were any at the time. Thus, if he is a Christian, writing for other Christians, the whole procedure can seem to be in-house, without impact on those who are not Christian believers. "The unbeliever in the fullest sense—the out-and-out atheist—is unlikely to have come Anselm's way."[11]

G. R. Evans devotes a chapter to this question, and she says that, in later years, Anselm would have encountered at least some *infideles*. They are even given parts in such dialogues as *Cur deus homo: Why did God*

---

10. G. R. Evans, whose little book *Anselm and a New Generation* (Oxford: Clarendon Press, 1980) is generally so helpful, oddly remarks about the *Proslogion* proof, that "the Fool is not to be taken seriously precisely because he is too foolish to know what he is saying. Anselm found it inconceivable that anyone who gave serious thought to Christian doctrine could fail to be orthodox in his beliefs" (p. 34). While God's existence is presupposed by orthodox Christian doctrine, it is something that non-believers might either affirm or deny.

11. Ibid., 34.

become man? But it is one thing to say that Jews reject the Incarnation and quite another to deal with the denial of God's existence. Evans does observe, without exploring the fact, that when a Christian and Jew disputed they could lay alongside their views those of the philosophers. It seems restrictive to suggest that Anselm had to meet atheists in order to understand the philosophical weight of the denial that God exists. Nor does it seem at all adequate to his effort to say that he was simply providing believers another way to think about their beliefs. Why avoid what seems on the face of it obvious? Anselm's proof was meant to reduce to incoherence anyone who denied that God exists. The psalmist triggered the effort but does not of course provide the proof that Anselm devised. If the proof works, it works for Christian and Jew, Muslim and pagan, not because they are any of these things, but because they are human beings with the ability to think. Doubtless it is the fact that this reasoning took form within the ambiance of Anselm's faith that causes the misunderstanding, but that is something we have already touched on and to which we shall return.

God Is Dead

We have recalled that the Father of Modern Philosophy, René Descartes, as well as Blaise Pascal, saw their philosophical work within the ambiance of their Christian, indeed Catholic, faith. Descartes's dream in 1619 and Pascal's mystical experience in 1654 are religious experiences. Descartes took his dreams to provide a sanction for his subsequent efforts to reform philosophy and to prove the existence of God. Pascal took his experience to underscore the fact that the God the philosophers spoke of and whose existence they sought to prove is not the God of religious belief. In the twelfth century, religious belief provided thinkers, as it had for Descartes and Pascal, the ambiance of their thought. Was the Father of Modern Philosophy less of a philosopher for this? It could be argued that throughout history the vast majority of philosophers have been theists or religious believers. It would be more difficult to argue that of the present batch of philosophers, of course. Among philosophers nowadays, at least, atheism is, if not the default position, the end to which anyone who seriously uses his mind is expected inevitably to come.

A. N. Wilson has recently published a book which takes its title from a poem of Thomas Hardy, "God's Funeral."[12] In it Wilson passes in review various nineteenth-century figures whose faith slipped away under the pressure of new knowledge that was taken to be incompatible with the faith. By and large, this meant the change by which one passed from having thought or held or believed p to be true, to holding, whether reluctantly or triumphantly, that p is false because we now know that $\sim p$ is true. But, as we saw in the previous lecture, this was to give way to another and far more vertiginous transition.

The passage in which Friedrich Nietzsche speaks of the death of God involves a madman. It is a madman or fool who stumbles into the marketplace proclaiming that God is dead and we have killed him. He is foolish because he thinks that God is the sort of being who can cease to be, whose life can be terminated by a human assassin. But the message, however madly put, is rightly taken to be Nietzsche's own. For us nineteenth-century Europeans, Nietzsche is saying, God no longer exists, he is as if dead, he is absent. It is because Nietzsche does not say that "God exists" is false that he can move us beyond true and false, beyond good and evil.

Many nineteenth-century figures came to think that evolution or some epistemological innovation or other had suddenly rendered all religious and indeed theistic claims false. There is nothing new in this sort of clearing-the-decks. We have seen that it characterizes modern thought. Step one is to kill off all surviving forebears, convict them and all preceding generations of elementary mistakes, and consign the lot of them to the dustbin. Step two is the announcement that now we can seriously begin. . . Such radical departures have succeeded one another in seemingly endless series since Descartes. Perhaps Nietzsche did not want to be the latest entrant into the arena of philosophical patricide. He wanted to put an end to the whole business of thinking that there is something out there awaiting our conceptual grasp, that our thoughts and words have meanings because they stand in a relation to the things that are, that our moral judgments are right or wrong with reference to objective criteria. The scandal of the history of philosophy was not that so many have said false things so much as that they have all believed there were true things to say.

12. A. N. Wilson, *God's Funeral* (New York: W. W. Norton, 1999).

Until recently, few could find it in them to be as radical as all that. Now it has become *chic*. The effect of such nihilism on natural theology is that it can no longer be claimed that natural theology is false. But could it be said that any of its claims are true? To be told that one has as much right to engage in natural theology as to dismiss it, since neither the affirmation nor the denial of God's existence could be true, is not the sort of description of his task that any self-respecting natural theologian could accept.

What has to be done is to show that the nihilistic position—we will ascribe it to Nietzsche—cannot be sustained. In one way, this is quite easily done; in another, it is the most difficult and important task confronting the modern mind. How do you deal with a naysayer who will not say you nay?

NOVEMBER 2, 1999

Radical Chic

Vostra apprehensiva da esser verace
  tragge intenzione, e dentro a voi la spiega,
  sì che l'animo ad essa volger face;
e se, rivolto, inver' di lei se piega,
  quel piegare è amor . . .
                    Purgatorio xviii, 22–26

The turn toward the subjective on the part of Descartes initiated developments that led eventually to a fashionable nihilism among influential philosophers. Nietzschean positions, for which Nietzsche gave up his professorship and finally his reason, are now adopted by some in comfortable university chairs in what turns out to be a profitable career move. We have seen that the proponent of natural theology could take momentary if cold comfort from the nadir that has been reached. No one can accuse him of falsehoods anymore. But then again he can never claim to have attained truths.

There is no reality *sans phrase*, only interpreted reality, what we make of it. No claim can be made that what one says has the support of the way things are because we can only get at the way things are by knowing and interpreting them. The concept of truth as conformity of judgment with that of which it is the judgment is discarded—the supposed two *relata*, the terms of the relation, are really only one.

A few years ago, sophisticates in Manhattan gave cocktail parties for groups dedicated to terrorizing the country, blowing up buildings with real people in them, and avoiding baths. This was called radical chic by

Tom Wolfe. Beaming patrons in tuxedos, well-groomed women in expensive dresses, mingled with the tousled and scruffy guests. Perhaps this was meant to gain them a pass from the coming terror. It was an endorsement of nihilism. Philosophy itself has now become a form of Radical Chic. Academics holding down comfortable positions, underemployed, fly about the world to talk to one another and deny that there is a world to fly around or that anything they or anyone else might say makes sense.

SIC INCIPIT TRAGOEDIA HOMINIS MODERNI

The judgment of Cornelio Fabro that this development was latent in Descartes himself commends itself more and more. In any case, it would be folly for one to seek to elevate a natural theology on the philosophical base available today. Admittedly, in saying this I am according a central position to views I regard as destructive of the philosophical enterprise, and with devastating social and political consequences beside. No wonder Kolokowski spoke of metaphysical horror. It could be objected that there are other currents running. I myself have noted the intimidating use of "we" in modern philosophy. I can only respond to that criticism by the tack I propose to take now.

I propose to journey far into the pre-Cartesian past in order to address head on the assumption of the regnant nihilism. The problem is no longer which of contemporary styles of philosophizing one might choose. The problem is the very possibility of philosophy.

NIL NOVI SUB SOLE

Almost from its beginnings, philosophy has had to deal with its dark twin, sophistry. The quest for wisdom, the truth about the world and ourselves, meant the slow ascent along a path strewn with obstacles. A problem solved generated other problems. But one pushed on. It became clear that there was no shortcut up the mountain; that this was a lifetime's task. Along the way the form and nature of argument had been distilled from particular arguments and studied for its own sake. Reason is a powerful instrument, but only if it is used correctly. We all make mistakes, but the Sophist was the man who deliberately abused reasoning. Aristotle put it this way in his *Sophistical Refutations* (165a21): "For the sophist's craft is an apparent wisdom but not a real one, and the sophist is a money-maker by apparent but not real wisdom."

Sophists show up in many Platonic dialogues, and not merely as bit-players. By and large, the Sophist is presented as the embodiment of what happens when the love of wisdom is perverted into the will for power. Plato may be said to emphasize the moral defect of sophistry, whereas Aristotle was concerned primarily with its logical flaws. Some seven hundred years later, Augustine wrote the *Contra academicos* to confront philosophers who held that nothing could be known. It is significant that Augustine as a believer saw the importance of addressing this attack on reason.

It is not easy to gain an accurate picture of "the crowd of Sophists" as Socrates called them. The term soon became one of opprobrium, but there are scholarly studies which question whether Protagoras and Gorgias and Hippias were, well, Sophists. The dialogues of Plato that take their titles from historical Sophists vary in tone and treatment. It is often noted that, while the *Protagoras* makes its titular figure somewhat comic, not all the good lines are given to Socrates. But the doctrine attributed to Protagoras and discussed in the dialogue qualifies as sophistry in the pejorative sense. Here is how Plato summarized it in the *Cratylus* (385e ff.), "As Protagoras meant when he said that of all things the measure is man, that as things appear to me, then, so they actually are for me, and as they appear to you, so they actually are for you."

Whatever nice things might be said about Protagoras, this passage is the key to seeing sophistry as the opposite of philosophy. Protagoras was the first of the Sophists, but he might be called the first of the Pragmatists as well. He offered to instruct young men so that they could succeed and prosper in the city. But if his teaching was based on the doctrine attributed to him, the result could be little more than a house of cards. From antiquity it was seen that the maxim of Protagoras could not survive application to itself. In the *Theaetetus*, Plato shows the vulnerability of the position that 'true' means 'true for me' and not just true *tout court.*

Yes, and besides that it involves a really exquisite conclusion. Protagoras, for his part, admitting as he does that everybody's opinion is true, must acknowledge the truth of his opponents' belief about his own belief, where they think it is wrong. (171a)

If all beliefs are true for the one who holds them, another who says their opposites are true—well, the opposites are true for him. To adopt Protagoras' teaching as true is to deprive oneself of saying that its contradictory is false. Plato's discussion is just beginning at this point but his critique comes down to saying Sophists maintain that a proposition and its opposite can both be true—that both p and $\sim p$ are true. But of course, Protagoras does not set out to hold both that his position is true and that it is false.

One remedy to this difficulty is to change the subject and talk of other things. But that, as Aristotle famously showed, will provide no refuge.

To speak at all is possible only if words have definite meanings, one or a finite range of meanings. They cannot be taken to mean both what they mean and its opposite. (I set aside ironic usage.) The claim that opposites are simultaneously true cannot be made except by acting contrary to this assertion, where the meanings of the words and the import of the utterance are concerned; they at least cannot mean what they mean and also what they do not mean.[1]

That both Plato and Aristotle should have spent so much time discussing a claim that falls of its own weight may surprise us. Much of what they say when discussing Protagoras *et sequaces eius* sounds like a man explaining a joke to someone who has no sense of humor. Why does Aristotle devote so many pages, chapter after chapter of Book Four of the *Metaphysics*, to say nothing of his analysis of fallacies, *On Sophistical Refutations*, to a discussion of the denial of the principle of contradiction when the denial, if taken seriously, must be the opposite affirmation as well?

> . . . if these have such opinions and express these views about the truth, is it not natural that beginners in philosophy should lose heart? For to seek the truth would be to follow flying [ever elusive?] game. (1009b36 ff.)

---

1. "Again, if all contradictory statements are true of the same subject at the same time, evidently all things will be one. For the same thing will be a trireme, a wall, and a man, if of everything it is possible either to affirm or to deny anything (and this premiss must be accepted by those who share the views of Protagoras)" *Metaphysics* iv.4.1007b18–22.

Protagoras and his ilk poison the well. To leave him unanswered would seem to be an acceptance of his verdict on any doctrine.

CONSISTENCY AND ONTOLOGY

Kolokowski has observed that those who dispense with truth and anything that might be called epistemological realism are reluctant to dismiss the demands of consistency.[2] I seize upon this. Of course this reluctance could be explained as simply due to a demand of language, but this would concede the starting point of Aristotle's ultimate defense of the principle of contradiction. One does not say both "It is raining now" and, speaking of the same time and place, "It is not raining now." But, as Kolokowski has suggested, this could be explained in a meta-language. "The rules of the language do not allow the simultaneous affirmation of 'It is raining' and 'It is not raining.'" The principle of consistency would be a rule of language and not any claim about the way things are. Of course, most native speakers would assume that they are talking about the weather, not the language, when they say it is raining or that it is not raining. It is because rain and its absence at the same time and place are not simultaneously possible that the sentences expressing these relate to one another as contradictories. Logic, as Quine must have said, recapitulates ontology.

When Aristotle talks of the first principle—that is, the ultimate fall-back—he gives several expressions of it:

1. It is impossible to affirm and deny the same thing of the same subject simultaneously and in the same sense.

---

2. See *Metaphysical Horror*, 31. I do not mean to suggest that Kolokowski would agree with what I go on to say here. He explicitly denies what I affirm. Speaking of the necessity of the ultimate, he writes, "What is thus meant by the necessity of the *Ultimum's* existence is that this necessity is its own and not ours. Our logic discovers the self-contradiction in the Absolute's non-existence because its non-self-contradiction is actually there, and not vice versa. Of course, we cannot discover this self-contradiction without first relying upon our logical norms which are supposed to derive their validity from the source of their being; the never ending curse of the vicious circle does not cease operating here, as in the search of the ultimate foundation." Kolokowski is not the only one who sees that anti-foundationalism follows from the supposed autonomy of the logical vis-à-vis the real. But it is not the real that conforms to the logical but logic which reflects the real.

2. It is impossible for a proposition and its contradictory to be simultaneously true.
3. It is impossible for a thing to be and not to be at the same time and in the same respect.

Thomas Aquinas, like Aristotle, uses these three as if they were synonymous. When he is speaking of the first principles of practical reasoning, the precepts of Natural Law, he draws an analogy between them and the first principles of reasoning as such. He gives as the most fundamental judgment reason makes, *non est simul affirmare et negare* (*ST* 1–2.94.2). That is Aristotle's first expression [1. above] of the principle: it is impossible to affirm and deny the same thing of the same subject simultaneously and in the same sense. But it is we who affirm and deny, so this is something *we* cannot do.

If I should say that Jorge Garcia both is and is not a gentleman, you will take me to mean that in some respects he is and in other respects he is not a gentleman. But if I should say that is *not* what I mean, I mean he is and is not everything a gentleman is supposed to be, the exchange would lose interest for you. You would think, perhaps even say aloud, "That's nonsense." I reply that that is what I say because that is what I think. Perhaps I might soften the blow by saying that this is the only exception to the principle I would urge. You would have to know Jorge to understand. But the rule is exceptionless. Why? To say that a proposition cannot be simultaneously true and false makes the point differently, let us say semantically. But neither (1) nor (2) will have any bite independently of (3).[3]

What exactly is the relation between (1) and (2) and (3)? If (1) expresses a psychological impossibility and (2) a logical impossibility, are they in some way *derived* from (1). The question takes its interest from the fact that we are speaking of first principles which, by definition, are underived.

> From the fact that it is impossible for a thing to be and not to be, it follows (*sequitur*) that it is impossible for contraries to be in the same subject simultaneously . . . and from the fact that contraries cannot simultaneously

---

3. I discussed these matters earlier in an essay called "Ethics and Metaphysics," which has become chapter 10 of my *Aquinas on Human Action: A Theory of Practice* (Washington, D.C.: Catholic University of America Press, 1992), 193–206.

inhere in the same subject, it follows (*sequitur*) that a man cannot hold contrary opinions, and consequently (*per consequens*) that contradictories cannot be thought to be true. . . .[4]

What is meant by *sequitur* and *per consequens* in this passage of Aquinas? The first principle by definition cannot be demonstrated, but here we have three expressions of it, and two are said to derive from the third. Clearly this derivation must be something short of demonstration. But it *is* discursive. The first and foundational judgment of human thinking can be expressed in terms of the fact that the things we know, *in rerum naturae*, are such that they cannot simultaneously exist and not exist. Since our knowledge is of reality—we do not first know our thinking or our expression of it—propositions will reflect this, and contradictories cannot simultaneously be true because this would involve the assertion that a thing can both be and not be at the same time and in the same respect. That is why we cannot hold contrary opinions. The derivations and sequences in the passage express the fact that our knowledge and language are of reality, and there is an order among them. It is this that prevents the principle of contradiction from being first of all a logical principle or a principle of language whose relation to reality is considered problematic. Logic and epistemology recapitulate ontology.[5]

To handle the persistent naysayer, Aristotle thought that ultimately it is necessary to point out that he must take his words to mean something and not anything or everything. And so must the one to whom he speaks. Suspecting that this commits him to the principle he denies, he might deny this as well. In doing so he simply removes himself from any

4. Thomas Aquinas, *In IV Metaphysic.*, lectio 6, n. 606.
5. Needless to say, this does not prevent the logical and epistemological from having characteristics of their own which reflect our way of thinking about reality rather than the characteristics of the real itself. The seemingly endless discussion of the Problem of Universals is only resolvable when one distinguishes first and second intentions. Predicable universality—to be said of many things—is not a feature of things as they exist, but of things as we know and speak of them. In grasping the nature of human individuals, we form a concept which expresses something found in each of the singulars. The noun expressing the nature is predicable of them all. Is human nature universal? As conceived and named by us? Yes. In itself? No. As found in Socrates and Xanthippe and other individuals? No. Logic rides piggy-back on reality without its elements being in one-to-one correspondence with the units of reality. But it is because of the dependence of our knowledge on the real that non-contradiction enters logic and acquires the antiseptic form $\sim(p \sim p)$.

sensible discussion, since his rejection of this requirement of language involves the principle he purports to deny as much as the acceptance of it would have. This kind of discourse is not the same as that involved in seeing the relationships among the three expressions of the first principle. This looks a lot more like an argument, and it is. But it is not a *demonstration* of the first principle.[6]

Aristotle's understanding of the various expressions of the first principle as well as his defense of it against the sophistic rejection of it, reposes on cognitive realism and a corresponding account of language. The primary objects of thinking and speaking are things themselves, not thinking or speaking about things themselves. The fundamental principle of reality, that a thing cannot exist and not exist at the same time, has its counterparts in our thinking and speaking.

Nowadays many philosophers reject the dependence of truth claims on reality and have developed theories of language to adjust to this denial. The Aristotelian response is not that each and every sentence is meant to express the way things are, and never the way we think or speak of them. But sentences about the way things are are paradigmatic. *The cat is on the mat. The fat is in the fire. The frost is on the pumpkin.* We don't always say such things—in actual fact we do not always speak grammatically or in complete sentences. Sometimes we ask questions or exclaim or express our wishes, sometime we praise or beseech. Sometimes we speak of nouns or verbs, sometimes of ideas and judgments and arguments. Far from ignoring this, the classical theory was the first to point it out. But it concentrated its attention on judgments and statements susceptible of truth or falsity.

Contemporary anti-realism cannot admit a sub-set of sentences expressive of the way things are. What is currently called pragmatism can be seen as an effort to generalize over all language what is true of some uses of language in the practical order. If that be so, it may be that cognitive anti-realism, insofar as it speaks the truth at all, has in mind something closer to practical truth in the old-fashioned sense.[7]

---

6. "Sed tamen hoc non erit demonstrans praedictum principium simpliciter, sed tantum erit ratio sustinens contra negantes. Ille enim qui 'destruit rationem' idest sermonem suum, dicendo quod nomen nihil significat, oportet quod sustineat, quia hoc ipsum quod negat, proffere non potest nisi loquendo et aliquid significando" (*In IV Metaphysic.*, lectio 7, n. 611).

7. See *Nicomachean Ethics* 6.2.1139a26 and Thomas on this text as well as in *Summa theologiae* 1–2.57.5.*ad* 3.

Nihilism as a Form of Sloth

Sloth or *acedia* is one of the capital sins and thus appears as a cornice on Mount Purgatory. Dante devotes Cantos 18 and 19 to it. Thomas defines it as weariness with acting well and sadness about spiritual things. While its primary form, as a capital sin, lies in not wanting to think about the divine good, not just any spiritual good, it can be extended to the intellectual life as such, the ultimate objective of which is knowledge of God.[8] Cassian speaks of it besetting monks in choir, usually in the sixth hour.[9] It seems to be a question of familiarity breeding boredom, if not discontent. Similarly, long years spent in pursuit of knowledge, in the fashioning and critique of argument, can lose their savor. As the monk is tempted to find the worship that is his *raison d'être* tiresome, so the philosopher can begin to feel a distaste for a pursuit that seems endless. He may begin to feel that *misology,* contempt for the Ideas, of which Plato speaks. And just as proper old ladies sometimes emit a vulgarity, to their own and others' surprise, and to their own at least momentary delight,[10] so philosophers can begin to undermine their own discipline and argue in order to destroy the point of arguing at all. Perhaps only a Dante could give an adequate account of the contemporary philosophy that considers itself the cutting edge, and which is dedicated to destroying philosophy.

It is not insignificant that the first move in this direction was taken in moral philosophy. Since moral judgments cannot be understood simply as a descriptive account of an empirical state of affairs, the question arose as to what moral terms mean. Ayer had already suggested the answer that gained in vogue. Moral terms are expressive of our subjective feelings, our emotions. Charles Stevenson gave a lengthy account of this theory of the meanings of *good* and *bad, ought* and the like, and called it Emotivism. If I find a state of affairs repellent, I disapprove of

---

8. Actually, sadness and boredom about lesser goods is extended to sadness concerning the highest spiritual good, so in the order of naming my application of *acedia* may take, if not pride of place, at least a place prior to the special sense of the term. Cf. *ST* 2–2. 35.1.

9. In his *De institutis monasteriorum* 10.1, cited by Aquinas in *Summa theologiae* 2–2.35.1, obj. 2. Cassian explains that the fasting monk, about noon, because of hunger and the position of the sun, feels sadness, and this may lead him to disdain the practice of prayer and its point, and that is sinful.

10. I think of Sartre's example of the Parisian matron who suddenly burst out into uncustomary profanity and afterward said, "I think I may be becoming an existentialist."

it. You may approve of it. Nothing in the state of affairs grounds either your reaction or mine.

This is not a theory that would occur to anyone unprompted by philosophical trends, save in special circumstances. In polite society, we do not elevate our preferences into absolute canons of taste. *De gustibus non disputandum est* remains a good rule of social intercourse. In many cases, "Chocolate ice cream is good" means only "I like it," and its denial "I don't care for it." These are sufficient and terminal when it is a question of flavors of ice cream and brands of beer. But it would be difficult to reduce our uses of *good* and *evil* to such cases, or to generalize from them over all uses of the so-called moral terms. But this was done, largely out of fear of the Naturalistic Fallacy, so named in 1903 in Moore's *Principia Ethica,* but having its roots in David Hume. The supposed independence of Ought from Is, of the prescriptive from the descriptive, precluded appealing to the way things are as the basis for our moral discriminations. The upshot is that we never *discover* the goodness or badness of types of action; we *confer* these qualities on them.

THOMAS REID AND THE SIGNS OF THE TIMES

One finds a parallel to the Aristotelian handling of those who would undermine the very foundation of human life in Thomas Reid. Reid considered the skepticism of his fellow countryman David Hume, not as an isolated aberration, but as the ultimate consequence of what had begun with Descartes. Baruch Brophy gives as the premises from which Reid saw Humean skepticism to follow logically, these:

i. The direct object of mental acts like perception, memory, and conceptions, are ideas in the mind of the perceiver, rememberer and conceiver.

ii. Philosophical arguments and proofs are needed in order to justify our belief in the existence of physical objects, the past, other minds, and the uniformity of nature.[11]

---

11. See Baruch Brophy's Introduction to his edition of *Essay on the Intellectual Powers of Man* (Boston: MIT Press, 1969), xvii. Brophy also introduced Reid's *Essays on the Active Powers of the Human Mind*, published by the same press in that same year.

Such representationalism as is expressed in *ii,* creates the insoluble puzzle of how we can get out of our minds to the things that at least some of our ideas stand for. Far from being given, starting points, we must prove the existence of the world, the past, other minds.

By contrast, Reid set out to show that such truths are in no need of being proved. He could not of course reject *ii,* as he did, and then go on to formulate proofs of the existence of the things on that list. What came to be called Reid's Common Sense Philosophy holds both that it would occur to no one but a philosopher to question the existence of such things, and that such non-gainsayable truths—he did not hesitate to call them self-evidently true—are the foundation on which truths that must be proved ultimately rest.

Of course there is nothing that we cannot discuss, and probably will, sooner or later. Reid could scarcely object to his predecessors pondering the matters he cites in *ii.* Those like Aristotle and Reid who call such truths self-evident go on and on about them, as the lengthy discussion of Book Four of the *Metaphysics* makes clear, but such discussion is far from skepticism. It is late in his *Essays on the Intellectual Powers of Man* that Reid takes up judgment.[12] It is Reid's contention that that which is commonly sensed is judged to be true. He spends a good deal of time contesting views which speak of the senses as bringing about ideas in the mind without any judgment being involved. He takes his to be the ordinary understanding of sense with which the philosophical is in disharmony. First principles are grasped by men with varying degrees of clarity or explicitness, but they do so because they are endowed with an inward light which, following Alexander Pope, Reid calls "a gift of heaven."[13]

It may be objected that Reid vacillates between using "common sense" to name a faculty or gift we all possess and to name truths which, thanks to this faculty, we cannot fail to know. But surely this is only a sign of the dependence of the former on the latter, *à la* Thomas Aquinas's discussion of Aristotle's various expressions of the very first

12. Essay VI, 532–709 in the edition cited.
13. From Pope's epistle to the Earl of Burlington, the relevant lines of which Reid quotes. See ibid., 558. One may be reminded of Johnson in the Preface to his *Dictionary of the English Language*: "I am not so lost in lexicography as to forget that *words are the daughters of earth, and that things are the sons of heaven.*" See *Samuel Johnson, A Critical Edition of the Major Works,* ed. Donald Greene (Oxford: Oxford University Press, 1984), 310.

principle. Indeed, Reid's first extended discussion of first principles comes after he has established the pedigree of his view and the way in which those who reject it have been unable to do so consistently, as when Hume "candidly acknowledges that, in the common business of life, he found himself under a necessity of believing with the vulgar."[14] Here is Reid's approach to first principles.

1. " I hold it to be certain, and even demonstrable, that all knowledge got by reason must be built upon first principles" (596).
2. ". . . some first principles yield conclusions that are certain, others such as are probable, in various degrees, from the highest probability to the lowest" (597).
3. ". . . it would contribute greatly to the stability of human knowledge, and consequently to the improvement of it, if the first principles upon which the various parts of it are grounded were pointed out and ascertained" (599).
4. ". . . nature has not left us destitute of means whereby the candid and honest part of mankind may be brought to unanimity when they happen to differ about first principles" (603).

Of course this is not a list of first principles, but statements about them. Nonetheless, in discussing 4, Reid invokes what Aristotle identified as the very first principle of all. Men do actually differ about first principles. "When this happens, every man who believes that there is a real distinction between truth and error, and that the faculties which God has given us are not in their nature fallacious, must be convinced that there is a defect, or perversion of judgment on one side or the other." This conviction, on both sides, arises from the implicit acceptance of $\sim(p\sim p)$.

But how precisely to adjudicate between claims that a given principle is a first principle? Reid refuses to leave this to an elite. Any one with a sound mind free of prejudice and who knows what is being asked can handle it?[15] One who denies a first principle will fall into absurdity

---

14. Ibid., 587.
15. "The learned and the unlearned, the philosopher and the day labourer, are upon a level, and will pass the same judgment, when they are not misled by some bias, or taught to renounce their understanding from some mistaken religious principle" (ibid., 604–605).

and become a rightful object of ridicule, wit and humor being other divine gifts to defend the gift of common sense. There cannot be any apodictical proof, but there are argumentative resources available as well as ridicule.

They are five: (a) The *argumentum ad hominem*, showing one's opponent to be guilty of inconsistency; (b) the argument *ad absurdum*, tracing the consequences of the denial to manifest absurdity; (c) the argument from authority; (d) from their presence from the beginning of our mental lives; and finally (e) from the practical absurdities to which their denial leads.[16] It is in discussing (c) the argument of authority that he gives us a list of first principles under the aegis of what all men have always believed.

> Who can doubt that men have universally believed in the existence of the material world? Who can doubt whether men have universally believed, that every change that happens in nature must have a cause? Who can doubt whether men have universally believed, that there is a right and a wrong in human conduct; some things that are entitled to approbation? (611)

Few readers fail to be impressed by Thomas Reid. They know he is right. Right in the way Chesterton was when he discussed what we mean when we call Dickens great. "But there is a third class of primary terms. There are popular expressions which everyone uses and no one can explain; which the wise man will accept and reverence, as he reverences desire or darkness or any elemental thing. The prigs of the debating club will demand that he should define his terms. And, being a wise man, he will flatly refuse. This first inexplicable term is the most important of all. The word that has no definition is the word that has no substitute."[17] Of course it would be a disservice to Reid to suggest that he sought to give his defense of common sense the same status as common sense itself.[18] My Thomistic regret about his discussion is his failure to

---

16. Ibid. These are to be found on pages 604 through 613.

17. G. K. Chesterton, *Charles Dickens* (London: Methuen, 1913), 9–10. When Aristotle discusses "act" and "potency," he does not define them but rather gives examples that help us see we already know their meanings.

18. Among the many helpful discussions of Reid, I shall mention only Lynd Forguson's *Common Sense* (London: Routledge, 1989), 103–127.

make the very first principle stand out from other first principles. If he had followed Aristotle's lead and concentrated on the first principle he would have been spared the carping criticisms of his various examples of lesser first principles.

The Cartesian turn led eventually, perhaps inevitably, to the present fashionable nihilism. That nihilism is reminiscent of nothing so much as the sophistry fought by Plato and Aristotle. Whether or no contemporary nihilists accept consistency—Kolokowski thinks they do—it is by reflection on the basis of consistency, the principle of contradiction, that one regains a correct understanding of the relation between words and thought and things in themselves. Once that has been reestablished, natural theology becomes a possibility. A disagreement between the theist and the atheist is possible, since one of them is right and the other is wrong. Atheists have as much stake in opposing the regnant relativism and nihilism as do theists.

NOVEMBER 4, 1999

LECTURE FIVE

Natural and Supernatural Theology

Per te poeta fui, per te cristiano.
Purgatorio xxii.73

When Dante and Virgil, his guide, come upon the Christian poet Statius in Purgatory, the poet gives the following description of the role Virgil played in his conversion.

> *Ed elli a lui: "Tu prima m'inviasti*
> *Verso Parnasso a ber ne le sue grotte,*
> *E prima appresso Dio m'alluminasti.*
>
> *Facesti come quei che va di notte,*
> *Che porta il lume dietro e sé non giova,*
> *Ma dopo sé fa le persone dotte."*
> *(Purgatorio* xxii.64–69)[1]

1. Then he: "Thou first didst guide me when I trod
   Parnassus' caves to drink the waters bright,
   And thou was first to lamp me up to God.
   Thou was as one who, travelling, bears by night
   A lantern at his back, which cannot leaven
   his darkness, yet he gives his followers light."

(Dorothy Sayers, *The Divine Comedy, II. The Purgatory* [London: Penguin, 1955], 242)

From the outset of the *Comedy*, Virgil functions as the pinnacle of human wisdom. He can guide Dante through the nether world of hell and up Mount Purgatory and to the very gates of heaven, but then his role is finished. For all his virtue and knowledge, Virgil was a pagan. Dante thus gives us a vivid image of the limitations of natural knowledge as well as of its relation to divine revelation. The Fathers spoke of pagan philosophy as a *praeparatio evangelica*, performing a role analogous to that of the Old Law in preparing for the New.

In preparation for his great poetic task, Dante devoted himself to the study of philosophy and theology. He studied under Dominicans, come to Florence from Paris, where they had been students of Thomas Aquinas. It is far from fanciful then to see Virgil as the symbol of natural theology. Moreover, his prominent role in this greatest of Christian poems suggests the continuing importance for believers of the kind of knowledge of God even pagans had.

NATURAL THEOLOGY AS MENACE

In the first lecture I alluded to Laurence Cossé's theological thriller in which an absolutely irresistible proof for the existence of God was shown to have social and ecclesiastical consequences of an unwelcome sort. While it is a great read, it relies on a conflation of a proof for the existence of God and proofs of the mysteries of Christianity. That is, of course, a conflation that is often made by those who feel faith is threatened by any effort to provide evidence for it. It will be worthwhile to consult Kierkegaard on the matter.

THE PHILOSOPHICAL FRAGMENTS

The Kierkegaardian literature comprises a number of pseudonymous works as well as works that appeared under his own name. These two groups relate to one another in ways Kierkegaard regarded as most important for an understanding of his overall literary effort. The overriding aim of the whole literature is to clarify what it means to be a Christian. That this should need clarification in a Christian country is due to the fact that nominal Christians understand their profession in ways which, according to Kierkegaard, fall woefully short of accuracy. Confusion or misunderstanding takes two general forms, and this explains the two movements in the literature, "Away from the poet!" and "Away from the philosopher!" Toward what? Towards a true understanding of what it means to be a Christian.

Kierkegaard assigns the task of dealing with the specifically philosophical misunderstanding of what it means to be a Christian to one pseudonymous author, Johannes Climacus, who functions in the literature somewhat as Virgil functions in *The Divine Comedy*. Two books are attributed to this author, *The Philosophical Fragments* and *The Concluding Unscientific Postscript to the Philosophical Fragments*.

The *Fragments* addresses itself to the following question: How far does the truth admit of being learned? Climacus, addressing philosophers, invokes the Socratic account of teaching as midwifery, the maieutic method whereby Socrates assists the learner in giving birth to an idea he already in some sense has. An analysis of this indicates that the Socratic teacher is not so much a cause as an occasion of learning in the pupil. The pupil is assumed to have the capacity to learn and learning is thus a transition from forgotten to remembered knowledge. The student does the learning or remembering and however much a teacher might be the occasion of this coming about, it is not *owed* to the teacher. Furthermore, the time when this takes place is not essential, but merely incidental. It would not matter if one proved a given geometrical theorem on Tuesday or Wednesday or that the work is not due until Friday.

Climacus may seem to be speaking of a very special account of learning, the Platonic, such that what is here said applies only to it. But it is clear that the Platonic account is taken to stand for any other. This is so because Climacus reduces the characteristics of Socratic teaching to three elements which are taken to show up in any account of learning.

1. The teacher is an occasion and not a cause.
2. The student has the capacity to learn and does not receive it from the teacher.
3. The moment when learning takes place is incidental to what is learned.

Any account of how it is that one person can help another come to knowledge of the truth will embody these elements.

Climacus now introduces a thought experiment. If the Socratic teacher is as described, what would a non-Socratic teacher be like? It is not immediately clear to the reader why this question should be pursued, but the reader is a philosopher and accustomed to pursue questions of no immediate practical significance. The simplest way to arrive at what a non-Socratic teacher would be like is of course to negate the features of Socratic teaching.

1. The non-Socratic teacher is the cause and not merely the occasion of the student's learning.
2. The non-Socratic teacher does not assume the capacity to learn, but gives the student this capacity.
3. The moment at which learning takes place is essential and not incidental to it.

In developing these, Climacus introduces terms which catch the reader's attention. The learner, not having the condition, is said to be in a polemical relation to the truth. Call this sin. The teacher in giving the condition as well as the truth saves the learner from error and sin. Call him a redeemer. The moment at which this teacher appears can be called the Fullness of Time. And so on.

Thus indirectly Climacus has drawn a contrast between any human teacher and Christ. He imagines his reader indignant with him for palming off as imaginary what we all recognize. The reader feels toyed with. Doubtless such reactions are particularly to be expected of a reader who had been thinking of Christ as a Socratic teacher and his teaching as just another instance of the sort of thing philosophers deal with. But if Christ is the non-Socratic teacher, so to think would be confusion. One might even have begun to think that Christianity was an invitation to understand on a par with any other philosophical teaching. On that understanding, ordinary cognitive equipment should suffice to determine its truth or falsity. The point of the contrast between the Socratic and the non-Socratic teacher is to induce doubt in the reader as to such reductionism.

Climacus never mentions Christ. Climacus never argues that there is a non-Socratic teacher. The impact of the book depends on its Christian reader remembering what he supposedly believes and then seeing that this prevents him from thinking of Christ as a Socratic teacher. To be a Christian does not mean to understand Christianity as if it were just another philosophical doctrine.

Anyone who thought himself a Christian and had a minimal grasp of Christian doctrine and who had adopted Hegelian or Kantian approaches to Christianity would, Kierkegaard assumes, be disturbed by this juxtaposition of the Socratic and non-Socratic teacher. Any effort to see Christ as merely another human teacher, that is, as a Socratic teacher, his doctrine within the limits of reason alone, would have to overlook basic Christian doctrines. Human beings are not in possession of the truth or capable of attaining it on their own: the truth about themselves—that they are wounded by sin and need a redeemer to free them from it—is not naturally accessible. Any attempt, accordingly, to make Christianity a doctrine among others, assessable by the usual criteria, amounts to the abandonment of Christianity.

Such indirect communication only works on the assumption of the last paragraph. The non-believer may find in this the confirmation of his worst fears about Christianity. One could grasp the concept of the non-Socratic teacher and have no reason to think it instantiated. But if one is a believer, the *Fragments* could have the effect of making him see that Christian doctrine is not just another philosophical doctrine and cannot be appraised by philosophical criteria.

WHAT IS RIGHT ABOUT THIS

If the Christian mysteries are truths which can be seen to be such only on the basis of faith, that is, trust in the God who reveals them without the ability in this life to comprehend those mysteries, then, by definition, any effort to prove the mysteries to be true by appeal to starting points in the public domain must fail. This does not mean that reason goes on holiday where faith is concerned. One of the convictions of the believer is that nothing he believes can be in conflict with what he knows to be true. That is, the principle of contradiction remains operative. So too, in arguing that some things that are revealed entail something else, one must abide by the common rules for valid reasoning. And of course the language of revelation is a language already in use, the words already have familiar meanings, so in one sense anyone who knows the language knows what it is being said. Without such knowledge, one could not reasonably accept or reject what is claimed. But the content is such that its truth or falsity cannot be definitively shown from what we know about the world. In this sense, the content of the mysteries of faith floats free of the reach of reason and it is a mistake to seek to prove it to be true.

A QUESTIONABLE EXTENSION

But neither Kierkegaard nor Johannes Climacus is a Thomist. Kierkegaard at least is a Lutheran and he has his pseudonym extend the strictures against presuming to understand Christianity to the point of vetoing any effort to attain knowledge of God's existence and nature. In short, the critique of the *Fragments* becomes a rejection of natural theology. This is to be found in Chapter III of the book.

The unknowability of God is founded on the notion that God is the Unknown. Of course this makes Climacus's claim seem merely tautological. He commends it to us by suggesting that the passion of reason is to will its own downfall, to come upon something that it cannot know. The Unknown thus haunts the realm of knowledge. This is not merely the banal claim that we know what we know and do not know what we do not know. Things we do not know may simply be things we do not yet know. But is there something that in principle we cannot know? We can tag it and call it the Unknown. And we can say we know what the term means—we have just given a descriptive account of it—but how do we know it refers to anything? For reasons that emerge Climacus bypasses this.

At the moment, he provides an analogy. Just as reason desires its own downfall and longs for the Unknown, so love passes from self-love to self-denial and is lost in the Beloved. The passionate paradox of reason thus recalls the paradox of love. But how do we know that the Unknown exists?

In the course of all this, another name for the Unknown is said to be God, so we have been brought to the question as to whether or not God's existence can be proved. Climacus takes a breathtaking route.

The existence of God cannot be proved because it is impossible to prove the existence of anything. Any supposed proof of the existence of X presupposes the existence of X. That is the Climachean claim. He applies it to traditional efforts to prove the existence of God. To say that the order of the world is a basis for coming to knowledge of God is to overlook the fact that the claim that there is an order already entails an orderer. One is begging the question of the existence of God.

Such criticisms are not peculiar to Climacus and there are of course responses to them. One could easily get bogged down in a seemingly endless discussion of traditional proofs. That is why the generalized claim is important, since it enables Climacus to free himself of particular discussions of proofs and sweep the board clean of all efforts to prove the existence of anything.

But is it true that any proof for the existence of X presupposes X? In some sense, obviously. That is, we must know what we are looking for, what X is taken to be. If X is a star thought to exist at such and such a location in the skies, we can understand the claim. But is there such a star? Why would the question arise? If it is merely a logical possibility, we can understand the claim but have no reason to give it more thought. If however the putative existence of the star is based on certain observable phenomena, the question is more interesting. Let us imagine that these are taken to provide reasons for thinking there is such a star, but the clincher will be when it is actually observed—in the way in which stars are actually observed. One night it is indeed observed.

This sketch, appropriately developed and made clearer, could count as the proof of the existence of the star. Prior to the proof, I have to know what I am looking for. The star is known through a description. But does that description describe anything? When we know that it does, we can say we have proved its existence. Knowing its description no more begs its existence than knowing that the happenings in the world are not merely random begs the question of God's existence.

I think it can be safely said that this is not at all the response Kierkegaard is looking for. His intention is that Climacus should simply sweep aside the whole business of natural theology and make efforts to know God's existence and nature equivalent to efforts to comprehend the mysteries of the faith. If he fails in this conflation, he nonetheless can represent all those believers who reject natural theology as a presumptuous effort. "Beware lest you be led astray by philosophy," Paul's admonition to the Colossians, might serve as Johannes Climacus's motto.

The Way of Subjectivity

Behind this dissatisfaction with proofs of God's existence lies a more profound objection. It seems to be in the nature of proof that it is impersonal, antiseptic, addressed to whom it may concern. One might fashion an objection similar to those Climacus makes against proofs of God's existence. Even if they worked, what real difference do they make? Christianity addresses us in the deepest well-springs of our being. The addressee senses that if Christianity is true, if he should give his assent to it, then his life must change. But proofs seem to address simply the mind. One might accept them and still be unchanged.

Of course this recalls the controversy that is as old as ethics itself. Is moral knowledge sought in order to be good? If it is practical knowledge, it should have practical import. Yet Aristotle says that no one becomes good by philosophizing. Plato, on the other hand, pays much attention to the claim that knowledge is virtue. If you really know what you should do, wouldn't you do it? And if you don't, can you really be said to have known what you should do? No wonder an analogy is drawn between the ethical and the religious.

The subjective approach to God, as found in Cardinal Newman as well as Kierkegaard, is something I shall turn to in my second set of lectures.

The example of Johannes Climacus makes clear once more that opposition to natural theology is perhaps more spirited on the part of some Christian believers than it is when it comes from the more or less blasé secular philosopher. The aim of such believers is to protect knowledge of God from philosophy. The only access to God is by faith and it is hubristic, even sinful, for us to presume that we can close the gap between heaven and earth by argument. Only if God comes to us can we go to God.

A first response to this would be intramural, citing passages of Scripture which seem clearly to say that sinful man, e.g., the pagan Romans whose misbehavior Paul catalogues, can come to knowledge of the invisible things of God by way of the things that are made. That Christianity depends essentially on things we already know is clear from the very fact of Scripture. We are assumed to know the language in which it is written, or the one into which it is translated. That language had a vast variety of ordinary purposes before it was used to convey God's revelation to us. In the New Testament, a relationship is established between the cleansing effect of water and the cleansing of sin from the soul. The parables of course rely on our capacity to be moved from what we already know to what we could only know under the impetus of grace. The Incarnation itself is the most striking instance of the way God relies on what we can see and hear and the further significance of Christ's deeds and words which surpasses any natural understanding.

Praeambula fidei

Thomas Aquinas employs the same bi-level feature as that found in the Bible. Thomas lived at the time when the treatises of Aristotle were for the first time available in Latin. This belated arrival of the pagan Aristotle drew mixed reactions. For one thing, the curriculum of medieval education was made obsolete by the presence of so many works that did not fit into any of the liberal arts. Moreover, the liberal arts had stood for human wisdom and as a preparation for the study of Scripture. Thus, a *modus vivendi* had been established between secular and sacred learning. With the arrival of the integral Aristotle, the idea that the liberal arts were an adequate summary of human learning became untenable, and this threw into question the *modus vivendi* between the secular and the sacred. It is small wonder then that some sought to keep Aristotle from the schools. They were unsuccessful. Thomas probably studied Aristotelian logical works at Montecassino as a boy, and when he went to the University of Naples he might have become aware of the "new" Aristotle. As a young Dominican he had the great good fortune to study with Albertus Magnus in Cologne. Thomas's acceptance of Aristotle is manifest throughout his works but toward the end of his life—in answer to an anti-Aristotelian crisis—he wrote interlinear commentaries on twelve of Aristotle's treatises.

This is important because Thomas held that Aristotle's proof of a Prime Mover was valid and that this was a proof for the existence of God. That proof, found in Aristotle's *Physics,* is complemented by the description of God in the *Metaphysics* in terms drawn from human intellection. This led Thomas to make a distinction of utmost importance for my task. (I don't suggest he made it to make my task easier—we hardly knew one another—but it has that effect.)

Thomas came to see that among the things that God has revealed about himself in the Bible are things that philosophers have said about him. Pagan philosophers. Philosophers utterly uninfluenced by revelation. From this he concluded that there are two kinds of truth about God found in Scripture. On the one hand are a few truths that can be known by human reason; on the other are truths about God that can only be known by revelation and accepted as true by faith. Among the things that the believer believes about God are that he is, that there is only one God, that he is the cause of everything other than himself, that he is intelligent. But such truths are to be found in the pagan philosophers. Why have they been proposed for our belief if they can be known? Is it of any interest to any believer to hold such truths otherwise than on divine authority?

Only if some truths about God can be known by unaided natural reason is this distinction possible. As a lifelong student of Aristotle, Thomas was convinced that there are sound and cogent proofs of God's existence. For Thomas, natural theology is not a possibility. It is a fact. It is the achievement of pagan philosophy. *Ab esse ad posse valet illatio.*

In one of his earliest works Thomas coined a phrase to cover these naturally knowable truths about God that had nonetheless been revealed. He called them *praeambula fidei.* They were distinguished from the other sort of truth about God, the kind that dominates Scripture, which he dubbed *mysteria fidei.* Thus it is that the task of natural theology can be described as the task of studying the Preambles of Faith.

Further discussion of this distinction must await the set of lectures I will give in February. I will close by noting how this distinction between *praeambula fidei* and *mysteria fidei* takes us back to the theme of the first lecture, the relation between the religious faith of the philosopher and his philosophizing.

Clearly, only a believer would think to call what pagan philosophers came to know about God preambles of faith. Just as only the early Christians who had studied philosophy before their conversion would refer to that philosophy as a Preparation for the Gospel. These are both extrinsic denominations. But they serve to locate within the ambiance of faith the philosophical task. One who like myself adopts the traditional reading of Romans 1:19 that I sketched a moment ago will see how that text sustains a believing philosopher when the going gets rough. Such a Christian philosopher is not likely to despair of the possibility of natural theology, whatever his personal setbacks. This extra-philosophical, pre-philosophical confidence brings him back to shoulder the task once more.

Thomas took note of the difficulties of that task, and of the flaws in its performance by pagan philosophers. He noted that the difficulties of natural theology make it unlikely that many will succeed at it and those who do will usually have reached a ripe old age. Knowledge of God is wisdom and thus is the culminating task of philosophy, of human learning. It is from such observations that Thomas drew his argument for the practical necessity that these naturally knowable truths about God be included in revelation. In this way, what was striven for by the pagan sages is put immediately into the possession of the simple as well as the not so simple.

It is clear that Thomas did not see natural theology as a threat to the faith. *Au contraire.* Moreover, his distinction between preambles and mysteries of the faith as subsets of revealed truth provided him with the means to fashion a powerful argument for the reasonableness of the believer's accepting as true what he cannot understand, for example, the Trinity, the Incarnation, the forgiveness of sin. For reasons we will discuss later, these mysteries cannot be *known* to be true; they cannot be proved from premises expressive of what we know. Faith is a testing knowledge, the acceptance of things unseen. But is it not inhuman to accept what so escapes our power to know?

Thomas's argument for the reasonableness of belief in the mysteries of faith is this.

If some of the things that have been revealed can be known to be true—the preambles—then it is reasonable to accept that the others—the mysteries—are, as they claim to be, true.

This is not of course a proof of the truth of the mysteries of faith, but it does prove that it is reasonable to believe them to be true. And it indicates the continuing interest, even for believers, of natural theology.

NOVEMBER 9, 1999

PART TWO

The Recovery of Natural Theology

Aspects of Argument

Venus Observed

In October I sought to clear the ground for what I shall be attempting in these February lectures. If the epistemological and metaphysical assumptions of the classic proofs for the existence of God had been shown by modern philosophers to be faulty, there would of course be little reason to bother with proofs which for centuries were considered sound and valid. Kant taught that all of the so-called cosmological proofs are in reality only variations on what he dubbed the Ontological Argument, a label that is applied to Anselm's proof in the *Proslogion* as well as to proofs by Descartes and others. The trouble with the Ontological Argument, its critics say, is that it seeks to move from the order of thought to an ontological conclusion. The very idea of God is taken to be the guarantee that the idea is an idea *of God*. One begins in the mental order and argues that there is one, and only one idea, that requires an extra-mental counterpart simply on the basis of the content of that idea.

Kant himself stands in the tradition that can be said to begin with Descartes, what might be called the epistemological tradition. Having cast into doubt all claims to knowledge, Descartes found the fact that he was thinking indubitable and in considering the objects of thinking came upon the idea of God. He then showed to his own satisfaction that, since he himself could not be the source of that idea, because of the richness of its content, its cause must be God himself. Methodic doubt had led to the assumption that thinking is about thinking, the external world having been put in brackets or in escrow, and the first philosophical task was, in effect, to get out of one's head.

But this, we argued at length in October, is a fundamental error from which sprang not only skepticism about proofs for the existence of God but eventually a general skepticism or subjectivism. We traced some of the history of this turn-to-the-subject in both the theoretical and practical orders. Hume's fact/value dichotomy was given new life by G. E. Moore who held that traditional moral philosophy had rested on the fundamental mistake of believing that moral judgments are grounded in objective truth. He invented the Naturalistic Fallacy to describe the mechanics of this mistake. In the theoretical order, there are many who have taken Kant's phenomena/noumena split to entail that our knowledge can never be knowledge of the way things are. All knowledge is interpretation, that is, our construal or construction. It follows, then, that, whether we are speaking of so-called value judgments or any other judgments, our knowledge is of our knowledge and not of things in themselves.

Cornelio Fabro, speaking on behalf of the tradition, and Thomas Reid speaking on behalf of common sense, saw the Cartesian turn to the subject as leading necessarily to the results just sketched, that is, to subjectivism, relativism, nihilism, atheism. Obviously, unless and until one showed that the Cartesian turn and its aftermath are indeed mistaken, it would be impossible to fulfill Lord Gifford's hope and speak on behalf of natural theology. The upshot of our previous lectures was to restore a basis on which theists and atheists can meaningfully disagree. If theism is merely one subjective option and atheism another, there is little point in asking which of them is true, truth no longer being attainable by the human mind. And by truth I mean the grasp of things as they are.

How does one make appeal to objective truth something other than an option, with no more warrant than any other stance—this being the ultimate consequence of the Cartesian turn? If this cannot be done, again, the objective option is a subjective option and there is only one option not two. Or, there are only *options*. Consequently, the objectivity of thought had to be shown to be inescapable, thus undermining the subjective option and showing it to rest on an egregious mistake. Far from objectivity being a subjective option, the subjective turn was seen to involve an inexpungeable appeal to objectivity. Here I took my cue from Plato and Aristotle as they confronted the seemingly live-and-let-live dictum of Protagoras. What is one to make of a position that says that what I think is true is true for me and what you think is true is true for you? Plato took the obvious tack of asking whether the dictum could be applied to itself. If it could, the saying was both true and false. Aristotle developed this and showed that such a position cannot be coherently maintained. Neither Plato nor Aristotle thought they were *proving* the fundamental assumption of thought; rather, they were showing its inescapability by reducing its rejection to nonsense. On this seemingly slim accomplishment, such was my conclusion, we have a basis for considering anew the truth of theism and the falsity of atheism—or, of course, vice versa.

Needless to say, one experiences a heady feeling in sweeping from the board the basic assumption of modern philosophy, but I emphasize that the upshot of our inquiry thus far is simply that the discussion of natural theology, pro and con, remains a task to be pursued and has not been discredited by the now discredited modern turn. Needless to say, such preliminary inquiries could have been extended indefinitely. There are and have been many counterclaims to what I have concluded. Moreover, there are many disguised forms of subjectivity which consider themselves to be accounts of objectivity, that is, accounts of why it is that our thinking is not arbitrary, that there are standards it has to meet, that positions cannot be reduced to the options of the solitary individual, as if solipsism were the natural offspring of the Cartesian turn. And so on. But what Reid called "Representationalism," that is, the claim that our knowledge is about our knowledge, however disguised, is still rampant in many circles that consider themselves, and are considered by others, avant-garde.

Philosophy has become a boneyard. Having passed through the abattoir of doubt, linguistic reduction, and nihilism, philosophy is but a skeleton of its former self. No wonder. Modern philosophy began by describing man as a thinking substance whose flesh and blood were yet to be warranted. We have ended with *ossa disjecta*. Perhaps Dickens's Mr. Venus could hook them up again. As for myself, like the object of Mr. Venus's attention in *Our Mutual Friend,* "I do not wish to regard myself, nor yet to be regarded, in that boney light."

THE SCANDAL OF PHILOSOPHY

Nothing has fueled modernity in its many modes more than the undeniable fact that the history of philosophy sometimes looks like a horizontal Tower of Babel extending through the centuries. There seems to be nothing on which philosophers are not in serious disagreement. Speaking of others, of course, philosophers have observed that there is nothing so absurd that some philosopher has not maintained it to be true. Who cannot sympathize with the longing for some method or approach which would put an end to this once and for all? However, instead of seeking a quick fix we are better advised to practice a long patience. The proposal of a *mathesis universalis*, a calculus that would enable us to appraise substantive arguments in a quince, has only generated more disagreement.

But doesn't logic equip us with just such a ready way of assessing arguments? If the rule of *modus ponens* or *modus tollens* is violated we feel justified in simply rejecting a proposed argument. So too with the rules of syllogism and of other types of argument. If the conditions for a valid argument are not met we are justified in dismissing the putative argument. With the spread of formalization in logic it became clear that one did not have to know what the values of p, q, and r might be in order to assess arguments that took the form "*If p, then q, but q, therefore p.*" Or "*If p then q, but not-p, therefore not-q.*" The *Principia Mathematica* inspired Bertrand Russell to develop a philosophy of logical atomism. If all molecular propositions, however complicated, are truth functions of their ultimate constituents, atomic propositions, the identification of the values of atomic propositions promised a way out of the scandal of philosophy. This was the dream that A. J. Ayer popularized in *Language, Truth and Logic*. Russell considered atomic propositions to be truths about sense data; Ayer said more broadly that they are empirical truths. But, as critics pointed out, these claims about the values of atomic propositions are not truths of logic, but extra-logical claims which soon fell to a criticism not unlike that which Plato had leveled against Protagoras. The so-called Principle of Verification—that all truths are either logical tautologies or empirical truths—could not be successfully applied to itself, and thus had an air of improvisation or arbitrariness about it, thereby contributing to, rather than removing, the scandal of philosophy.

The negative criterion of formalism was one thing, but to seek to make logic positively decide the truth of the interpreted symbols for propositions is quite another. The language of logic—Russell called it a syntax without a vocabulary—is a second-order language. The medievals said logic dealt with second intentions, that is, with relations established by the mind between first intentions, which were grasps of the way things are. A logical analysis is always at one remove from talk about the things that are. For the medievals, this drew attention to the fact that logic rides piggy-back on our knowledge of the world. Logic could no more be the first thing we think about than could first intentions be the *object* of thinking in the sense of Reid's Representationalism. Thinking itself, like the relations established between things as we think about them, is a reflex object of thought, not its first object.

VIA MANIFESTIOR

There is no more famous text in discussions of natural theology—that is, philosophical efforts to prove the existence of God and establish certain truths about his nature—than the so-called *quinque viae* of Thomas Aquinas, five ways to prove the existence of God.

Dicendum quod Deum esse quinque viae probari potest. Prima autem et manifestior via est, quae sumitur ex parte motus. Certum est enim, et sensu constat, aliqua moveri in hoc mundo. Omne autem quod movetur, ab alio movetur. Nihil enim movetur, nisi secundum quod est in potentia ad illud ad quod movetur: movet autem aliquid secundum quod est actu. Movere enim nihil aliud est quam educere aliquid de potentia in actum: de potentia autem non potest aliquid reduci in actum, nisi per aliquod ens in actu: sicut calidum in actu, ut ignis, facit lignum, quod est calidum in potentia, esse actu

It should be said that there are five ways in which God can be shown to exist. The first and most obvious way is based on motion. For it is certain and evident to the senses that some things in this world are moved. But whatever is moved is moved by another. For something is moved insofar as it is in potency to that toward which it is moved, and something moves insofar as it is in act. To move is nothing other than to educe something from potency to act, and a thing can be brought from potency to act only by something in act, as fire causes wood which is only potentially warm to

calidum, et per hoc movet et alterat ipsum. Non autem est possibile ut idem sit simul in actu et potentia secundum idem, sed solum secundum diversa: quod enim est calidum in actu, non potest simul esse calidum in potentia, sed est simul frigidum in potentia. Impossibile est ergo quod, secundum idem et eodem modo, aliquid sit movens et motum, vel quod moveat seipsum. Omne ergo quod movetur, oportet ab alio moveri. Si ergo id a quo movetur, moveatur, oportet et ipsum ab alio moveri; et illud ab alio. Hoc autem non est procedere in infinitum: quia sic non esset aliquod primum movens; et per consequens nec aliquod aliud movens, quia moventia secunda non movent nisi per hoc quod sunt mota a primo movente, sicut baculus non movet nisi per hoc quod est motus a manu. Ergo necesse est devenire ad aliquod primum movens, quod a nullo movetur: et hoc omnes intelligunt Deum. . . . (*ST* 1.2.3)

be actually so, thus moving and altering it. A thing cannot be at once and in the same sense in potency and in act, but only in different respects: what is actually warm cannot at the same time be potentially so, though at the time it is potentially cold. It is impossible for a thing to be at once and in the same sense moving and moved. So whatever is moved is moved by another. And if that by which it is moved is moved it must be moved by another, and so on. But this cannot go on infinitely, for then there would be no first mover nor any other mover, because secondary movers move only insofar as they are moved by the first mover, as a stick moves only insofar as it is moved by the hand. It is necessary, therefore, to arrive at some first mover which is not moved by anything else, and this is what all men understand God to be.

In its stark simplicity, the proof would be stated thus:

*Whatever is moved is moved by another.
*There cannot be an infinite series of moved movers.
*Therefore there must be a first unmoved mover.

Appraised formally, from the point of view of logic, this proof works. The problem thus becomes one of knowing whether the consequent is true, not whether it is truly consequent upon the premises. How is this to be decided? By finding out whether the premises from which it logically follows are true.

An unfortunate consequence of the favor shown this text in introductory philosophy classes is that the neophyte is apparently expected to decide whether it is a good proof, that is, decide whether its premises are true. The text occurs in the *Summa theologiae,* which Thomas wrote precisely for beginners, so this may seem fair enough. But the beginners for whom Thomas was writing were beginners in theology, not philosophy. Indeed as the very first question raised in the *Summa* indicates, its readers are assumed to be well-versed in philosophy.[1] And as philosophers, Thomas's theological beginners have already established the existence of God. They will know that Aristotle called the philosophical discipline that culminates the lengthy task of philosophy *theologia.* It has come to be called metaphysics, and is in effect the wisdom the seeking of which gives philosophy its name. The proof from motion is to be found, however, in natural philosophy, in Books 7 and 8 of the *Physics.* But the proof cannot be understood—that is, its premises cannot be judged true—except on the basis of everything that has preceded the proof in the *Physics.* In short, a proof which rides on a host of preliminary matters, could not be intelligently appraised by the student of philosophy at the beginning of his studies. This is why it is misleading to assume that Thomas presumed that beginners in philosophy are capable of an intelligent appraisal of the proof from motion.

What Thomas is doing in the *Summa* is sketching things his readers have already studied in detail. Why does he do that? Because he is concerned to compare what philosophers concluded of God by way of proofs with the truths about himself that God has revealed. Thus, in *ST* 1.2.2.*ad* 1*m* he observes that what can be known about God by way of natural reason, such as that he exists, is not to be counted among the things that are articles of faith; rather such truths are *praeambula ad articulos* and are among the naturally knowable things which are presupposed by faith, as grace presupposes nature. Of course such naturally knowable truths about God will first have been believed by Thomas's Christian readers before they fashioned a philosophical proof of them, but Thomas sees no difficulty in the same truth being held by demon-

1. The *Summa theologiae* begins by asking whether there is need for any science beyond those that make up philosophy. The question only makes sense to one who has a sufficient knowledge of philosophy to see the problem. Among the things that he is taken to have learned in philosophy is that the existence of God can be proved.

stration and by faith, since these are two quite different ways of holding it. He does not, however, think that the same truth can be simultaneously known and believed.

Furthermore, before sketching the proofs by way of reminder of what his reader will already have established demonstratively, he has some general things to say about the demonstrability of God's existence.

This discussion draws on his reader's knowledge of logic since, relying on Aristotle's *Posterior Analytics*, Thomas will distinguish between truths which are known in themselves—*per se*—and truths which are derived from other truths—*per alia*. God's existence is not self-evident, he notes, so if it is known, as opposed to believed, this must be by way of a demonstration. But demonstrations sometimes proceed from cause to effect, in what is called the demonstration *propter quid, of the reasoned fact*, and at other times proceed from effects to the existence of their cause—the demonstration *quia*. God can be philosophically known to exist only by means of a proof which takes its rise from his effects.[2]

These allusions to logic are also a reminder of what the reader of the *Summa theologiae* is expected already to know. My point here, then, is this. Proofs for the existence of God can neither be fashioned nor appraised without reliance on a vast fund of knowledge. Philosophy does not begin with such proofs, although it does begin in the hope that the natural hunch that God exists—which the philosophical neophyte, pagan or Christian, brings to his study—will turn out to be provable, and when it is, the wisdom sought, the *telos* of philosophy, will have been attained. The remarkable opening chapters of Book One of the *Metaphysics* suggest by way of a promissory note that our natural desire to know, shown to be a quest for causes, will reach its culmination in knowledge of the first cause of all the things that are.

Is this a begging of the question? If the inquirer were a solitary individual setting out without guide or mentor to satisfy his desire for knowledge it is perhaps doubtful that he would describe his interest in a lunar eclipse as leading inevitably to knowledge of the divine. But when it is a question of learning, of being taught, and not of discovery, the one teaching is presumed to have the knowledge he will eventually im-

---

2. In all this Thomas is guided by Romans 1:20 where Paul says of the pagan Romans that they could from the things that are made come to knowledge of the invisible things of God.

part to others.[3] One who is wise is instructing others on what wisdom is and how to attain it. His listeners must take his word for it at this juncture. *Oportet addiscentem credere.* Discovering on one's own and being taught by another have the same starting points however different the ambiance of instruction is from that of discovery. Some things are naturally known prior to inquiry; teaching addresses the knowledge the student already has and seeks to help him move on from that to what he previously knew only potentially. In short, teaching takes place against a wide and deep background shared by teacher and student, the culture within which they and countless others stand.

Following a Proof

When the proof from motion is reduced to the stripped down form we have given it, which is a simplification of a simplification, we would not of course think that the three sentences accomplish something of themselves. Language involves both a speaker and a listener, and a proof is the distillation of someone saying something to someone else in a given context. The proof is presented in such a way that its addressee can reenact the process captured by the written proof. It would be absurd to imagine that a proof need merely be stated in the presence of hearers in order to have the desired effect. It is addressed to someone on the *qui vive*, someone who wants to know, who can grasp the meaning and truth of the premises and thus, given the validity of the sequence, is enabled to see the truth of the conclusion. The logical appraisal of the proof may pay little or no overt attention to who is talking and who is the addressee and what is presupposed on either side. But since the logical appraisal leaves untouched the question of the truth of the premises, it must be regarded as relying on minimal and preliminary criteria.

From the beginning, philosophical reflections on language have made it clear that not every utterance is meant to convey a truth.[4] Speak-

---

3. Thomas makes this distinction between *inventio* and *doctrina* in his *De magistro*, *Quaestio disputata de veritate*, q. 11.

4. Contemporary philosophers must be grateful for the work of J. L. Austin in this regard. From *How To Do Things with Words* (Cambridge, Mass.: Harvard University Press, 1955) through *Sense and Sensibilia* (Oxford: Oxford University Press, 1964) as well as in

ers may be engaged in a variety of performances, sometimes exhortatory, sometimes asking a question, sometimes praying or making a promise. There are sentence forms which customarily convey this, but it is not necessary that the different performances be syntactically signaled. Nor does this usually present any problem to those conversing in a language both know. What is clear is that the appropriate response to what is said takes into account a vast number of things that go unsaid. If one responded to the speeches of actors on a stage as he does to remarks made on the street, breaking into Hamlet's soliloquy from the balcony in an effort to cheer up the poor prince, we would recognize that he needs help in distinguishing these two uses of language. Not every question a character asks is rhetorical, but the proper respondent is on the stage, not in the audience—*pace* Pirandello.

Reflection on the background assumptions of language makes it clear that it would be clumsy if a speaker sought to make these explicit whenever he spoke to another. In the kind of language that characterizes philosophical proofs, as Thomas has been recalling them, the speaker is presumed to be saying things about the things that are. His listener's attention, accordingly, is not being directed to what the teacher knows or thinks but rather to the things he himself knows. If in speaking of lunar eclipses, the teacher spoke in rhyming couplets or declaimed in the manner of an orator, this would distract attention from *what* he is saying to *how* he is saying it. Aristotle locates demonstrative philosophical language, the language used in the quest of truth about the things that are, on a spectrum which has as one of its extremes poetic language. In poetry the medium is a good part of the message, the music of language is not merely a means the poet uses to say what he has to say, it is integral to what he means. If we tracked back along this spectrum to what we might call the apodictic use of language, the music of what is spoken should become like the music of the spheres, inaudible. Horace said the best art does not call attention to itself, but this cannot be understood as meaning that Horace thinks his elaborate prosody is incidental to what he is saying. But he does not want his hearer to scan the verse as he is hearing it, although what he is hearing is, especially in the case of Horace, most artfully contrived.

Philosophical Papers (Oxford: Oxford University Press, 1970), he drew attention to much that had been overlooked.

It should not be concluded from this that the language of the philosopher is artless. *Au contraire.* The philosopher must be at great pains to use language as a pure medium so that it does not distract from what he could convey, which is a truth about the things that are. Brand Blanshard's work *On Philosophical Style* was once almost the only entry in a field that is more populated now.[5]

But if the aim of philosophical language is to fashion apodictic proofs, the way to such proofs involves discourse of various kinds. Aristotle's taking of geometrical proof as a kind of model of demonstrative reasoning in the *Posterior Analytics* has led to misunderstanding. Scholars have complained that Aristotle's carefully developed scientific methodology does not seem to characterize his procedure in the treatises. Because of its abstract character, Euclidean geometry—Euclid lived a century after Aristotle, but of course geometry did not begin with him—can proceed as it were *ab ovo*. Its reliance on our experience of the world is minimal. But a science of nature must undertake many preliminary analyses before anything like a demonstration can be offered. Thus, it has been said that the first demonstration in the *Physics* occurs in Book Three of that work. What then has been going on previously? Aristotle first reviewed what his predecessors had to say about nature and change and found beneath the apparent cacophony of voices a number of basic assumptions. This suggested to him that those assumptions are likely true. But he then proceeded to his own analysis of what comes to be as a result of a change and presents his famous claim that any change involves an abiding subject which from not having a certain characteristic comes to have it. This fundamental Aristotelian doctrine is not proved in the sense of demonstrated. It purports to be an analysis of what we already know which commends itself against the background of what his predecessors had to say. So too the discourse of Book Two does not demonstrate anything about the presumed subject of the science.

The differences between the procedures of geometry and natural science are due to their quite different subject matters and the accessibility of those subject matters to us. It is notorious that the procedure of the *Metaphysics* instantiates the methodology of the *Posterior Analytics*

5. The matter of these paragraphs is discussed in my Aquinas Lecture, *Rhyme and Reason, St. Thomas and Modes of Discourse* (Milwaukee: Marquette University Press, 1981).

only in the most remote way. As Aristotle remarked, it is the mark of the wise man to look for what the subject matter permits and not expect geometrical precision in every subject.

THE EFFECT OF A PROOF

Forgive me for dwelling on these commonplaces, but there is yet another I must mention. I have been speaking of discourse as it is to be found in what Aristotle called the theoretical sciences. When Aristotle distinguished mind theoretical from mind practical in his *De anima* (III, 10), he pointed to different aims of thinking. Sometimes we use our mind to find out what the truth of the matter is; sometimes we use our mind in order to have a guide for making or doing. Practical thinking reaches its end in something made or done. Theoretical thinking aims at the perfection of thinking as such, Truth.

Classical proofs for the existence of God are exercises in theoretical reasoning. If the learner reenacts the thinking embodied in the proof he will arrive at a new truth. That is the aim and end of the process. It is useful to recall this because one source of dissatisfaction with the classical proofs derives from the fact that a person might accept them and still live as if God did not exist. When one asks undergraduates whether they think God's existence can be proved they usually say No, and often this is because of their belief that, if the proof worked, it ought to change the life of anyone who accepted it.

This sets the stage for my next lecture which will deal with the distinction between changing one's mind and changing one's life.

FEBRUARY 8, 2000

Intemperate Reasoning

video meliora, proboque,
deteriora sequor
      Ovid, *Metamorphoses* vii.20 –21

I
n this lecture I discuss the difference between changing one's mind and changing one's life. The distinction is important for my purposes because one misgiving about classical proofs for the existence of God seems to be based on the assumption that, if they worked, the one who accepted them would exhibit this by a change in his mode of living. That this is an important and relevant objection is clear from the implication of the Pauline text on which the Christian tradition bases its confidence that the human mind can, by its natural powers, come to knowledge of God. In that first chapter of the Epistle to the Romans, Paul links a negative judgment of Roman morals (*inexcusabiles*) to the Romans' ability to achieve knowledge of God. Their behavior is inexcusable because they should know better, and since they can know that God exists they have a powerful reason for acting otherwise than as they do. The suggestion clearly is that such knowledge, knowledge gained as the result of a proof of God's existence, has moral implications.

THEORETICAL AND PRACTICAL REASONING

We have already referred to the *locus classicus* (*De anima* III,10) in which Aristotle distinguished the practical from the theoretical use of mind on the basis of their different aims or ends. When we put our mind to a practical problem—something to be done or made—the successful upshot of such reasoning should be the doing or making, not just thinking about them. The end of practical reasoning is thus beyond, over and above, the good of reasoning as such. The good of reasoning as such, the aim of the theoretical use of our mind, is the perfection of thinking as such, truth. It might be said, accordingly, that the aim of practical thinking is the perfection of some activity other than thinking itself.

There are other criteria for distinguishing theoretical and practical thinking which provide a finer grained understanding of their modulations and degrees. The end is the place to start, of course, because then we can ask what sorts of object of thought can be put to the different ends. Not everything we think about has practical import, at least not in any immediate way. The calculation that the sun is 93,000,000 miles from earth does not galvanize us into action as if it were a practical maxim. "What? That far? I'd better hurry." When the astronomer assigns that distance the value of 1 and calculates other celestial distances with it as yardstick, he may be said to be putting such knowledge to use, but the use to which it is put is the gaining of further knowledge. That such calculations become important when space probes are undertaken does not turn them as such into maxims or guidelines for acting. They retain their status as true propositions about the way things are. That practical guidelines may be formed on their basis is of course true and not irrelevant to all efforts to separate, as it is said, fact from value. And of course not irrelevant to the point of this lecture.

Truth is the primary value of thinking, the aim of the activity, its *telos*. Thinking aimed at an end other than truth is an extension of such primary thinking and presupposes it. It is because such-and-such is the case, that something may or must be done. Nothing is more familiar to us than this supposedly suspect discursive sequence. So also when we distinguish thought and action, we do not wish to deny that thinking itself is an activity (in a secondary sense) that precedes action in the regulative sense of choosing, moving about, making bird houses, and the like.

In the preceding lecture it emerged that, while we may think of a proof as a series of sentences on a page, they cannot as such prove anything, anymore than a musical score can fill the ear with sound. Someone seeks to prove and someone else attends to the proof. The prover seeks to have the addressee reenact in his own mind the process the prover has already gone through and which he is expressing by what he says. When the addressee re-enacts the process successfully, he has acquired true knowledge that he did not previously have. This does not of course mean that what the prover knows and proves is some process going on in his mind and what the learner comes to know is a process going on in *his* mind—or in the teacher's mind. The teacher's thinking is numerically different from the thinking of the learner, but when the process of proving succeeds, teacher and learner know the *same* truth. This may be taken to be a paradigmatic instance of the transfer of theoretical knowledge.

In calling knowledge theoretical we seem inevitably to be referring to a sophisticated activity, formally undertaken by those who have a special talent and opportunity for it. When Aristotle distinguishes the theoretical and practical sciences which make up philosophy, he is indeed referring to rather sophisticated accomplishments. But prior to theoretical and practical sciences, there is theoretical and practical thinking, and this is first of all of the most ordinary sort. *All men by nature desire to know.* Our initial resistance to this sweeping claim is due to the fact that many, perhaps most, people show little appetite for the kind of cognitive pursuits that characterize lecture halls and laboratories. But if that is true, the reverse is not. Sophisticated and professional thinkers have used, continue to use, and will always use their minds in the way that every human person does. Not all knowledge is science but science presupposes the kind of knowledge in which everyone engages. The theoretical knowledge that is found in the sciences is the fruit of and extension of the theoretical knowledge everyone has of the world around him and himself in it.

THEORETICAL THINKING AND THEORETICAL SCIENCE

The need to make this truism explicit will become clear as we proceed. We must not equate theoretical and practical thinking with theoretical and practical sciences, although the problem of this lecture arises from a scientific effort to prove the existence of God.

In order for our thinking to be immediately or as such (i.e., as thinking) relevant to action, its object must be something we can do or make. That was the point about the distance of the sun from earth. This is not a truth we can do anything about, it is not something we bring about. When I am thinking about a bird house or stealing your wallet, my mind is occupied with something I might make or do. But I can consider such things in a way that would seem indistinguishable from my consideration of things I cannot make or do. For example, I might describe and define a bird house in the same way that I would a robin's nest, as if it were simply an item in the natural world. And I might discuss an act of theft as a vicious act contrary to the cardinal virtue of justice in one of its more specific manifestations. Or I might describe it in a story. Such statements about make-able or do-able things would be assessed in the same way as statements about the things of nature. Either they are true or they aren't.

But there is also what might be called a practical way of considering such *agibilia* and *factibilia*. The book I bought—*How To Build a Bird House*—tells me what materials to buy and what tools to have on hand and then, in word and picture, it directs me through the steps which, when taken, result in a bird house. Thus to know something make-able, not in a way that seems indistinguishable from theoretical knowledge, but as the result of a definite series of steps, is to know it as make-able in a far stronger sense. Of course, I may have my feet up, my pipe lit, and be simply savoring the account of how I might make a bird house. I understand the steps, in mind and imagination I make them, perhaps, but my feet remain up and I continue to puff indolently on my pipe. How different is this knowing from that which would be embedded in my action if I had gone down to my work bench, followed the steps, and built a bird house.

Thomas Aquinas, on whose development of Aristotle I am relying here, isolated three criteria for practical knowledge. Practical knowing has as its object something make-able or do-able, one knows it in a practical as opposed to a theoretical way, and the end is the actual employment of this knowledge, which is revealed in the actual doing or making. This enables us to speak of degrees of practical knowing. When the object of our knowing is something make-able, but we are thinking of it as we would a natural thing—classifying, defining, etc.—this is practical knowledge in a minimal sense. To know such an object as the result of a series of steps is to have practical knowledge in a fuller sense. But practical knowledge in the fullest sense is that which is at play when one is working at his bench, actually directing the movements of hands, arms, etc. as they saw, hammer, and paint.[1]

OVID'S LAMENT

The most discussed instance of the relationship between understanding and performance lies in the moral order. Plato asked if one can become what one ought to be simply by taking the fifty drachma course. Is virtue learnable? This is a most agonizing problem for the philosopher, since it seems to call into question the primacy of thought, but it is one that everyone has doleful experience of.[2] Paul spoke of not doing the good that he would and doing the evil that he would not. Aristotle says that one does not become good by philosophizing and Thomas says of moral science that it is of little or no value for action.[3] The initial question and these surprising remarks point to a relationship between knowing and doing that has exercised philosophers almost from the beginning, and everyone else as well.

Kierkegaard tells the story of a recruit in ranks who is told by his sergeant to be silent. He replies by saying that he understands what the sergeant wants; he would like the speaker and all others not to speak in ranks. "Shut up!" explains the sergeant. "Ah yes," the recruit responds, "a command is unlike a question." The story is meant to illustrate the fact that we can understand yet by our actions show that we do not understand. The proper response to a command—in the Marines at least—is to obey it, not produce a gloss on it. So too the proper response

---

1. See my *Ethica thomistica*, rev. ed. (Washington, D.C.: Catholic University of America Press, 1997), 38–40.

2. See the famous lines from Ovid's *Metamorphoses* cited at the head of this chapter.

3. Aristotle, *Nicomachean Ethics* 2.4.1105b12–18: "But most people do not do these, but take refuge in theory and think they are being philosophers and will become good in this way, behaving somewhat like patients who listen attentively to the doctor, but do none of the things they are ordered to do. As the latter will not be made well in body by such a course of treatment, the former will not be made well in soul by such a course of philosophy." See Thomas's commentary, lecture iv, n. 288 and *Disputed Question on the virtues in general, a. 6, ad 1m.*

to a moral principle is to be guided by it in our behavior. Moral knowledge has good behavior as its aim. Is it possible to have true moral knowledge that does not achieve its goal?

The fact that we are as shocked as we are when those whose lives are defined in terms of conveying a moral message themselves violate that message suggests that we expect such knowledge to influence the behavior of the one who has it. How can one act contrary to the knowledge he has? It is tempting to think that if one's behavior is bad he cannot *really* know what we took him to know. On the other hand we have autobiographical experience of the fact that our own actions all too often diverge from what we know they ought to be. Indeed, it is difficult to know what acting badly would morally mean if it did not mean acting contrary to knowledge we are presumed to have.

KNOWING AND WILLING

It could of course be said that knowledge only takes us so far and then either our emotions or will takes over, that there is a leap from the cognitive order into the order of action. Then bad action could be blamed on the freakish operation of will rather than on a defect of knowledge. But if human action is voluntary and voluntary action is a knowing-willing or a willing-knowing, as Aristotle suggests of choice, the bad action like the good must have a cognitive component. If our choice is not governed by our true knowledge of what we ought to do, as a human choice it must be governed by a judgment contrary to that true knowledge.

Can we knowingly do the wrong thing? Aristotle suggests that it depends on what we mean by knowing. Sometimes one is said to know because he is capable of expressing a judgment but is not presently doing so. Someone sleeping on the beach might be said to know quantum physics; but obviously this means that if you wake him up and ask an appropriate question his knowledge could be actualized in his answer. One may be capable of knowing or he may actually be knowing. A second distinction is between knowing in general and knowing in the particular case. I may know and believe that fornication is wrong yet go on to commit a particular act of fornication. In order to do so my judgment that it is bad must be overridden by the judgment that it is good.

The former is the grasp of a general truth, the latter a particular judgment here and now.

Such distinctions enable Aristotle to say that we act contrary to our knowledge when our particular judgment here and now does not conform with our general judgment of what is right or wrong. But how can we make so elementary a mistake, that is, not identify a particular as an instance of a universal? Aristotle suggests the following model of practical discourse. We bring to a particular situation a fund of general lore as to how we ought to behave. This general lore conveys what is good for us, that is, what will really fulfill our will whose object is our good. On the level of generality, to know about the good is to have true knowledge about it, but the good is the object of desire, not merely an occasion for thought. Practical discourse involves the transition from knowledge of the good to the pursuit of the good known. One whose appetite is not inured to the good of temperance may have true knowledge of temperance and of rules for attaining and strengthening it, but when he seeks to act on this general knowledge the character he has as a result of previous intemperate choices intervenes and his here-and-now judgment is that the pleasure of the act suffices to choose it.

The reasoning of the intemperate man thus goes off the rails because the good he knows is not *his* good, that is, it is not what he habitually seeks. His actual choice is governed by a particular judgment, as is the choice of the temperate man, but the here-and-now judgment of the temperate man is in conformity with his general knowledge about temperance and its demands and that of the well-informed but intemperate man's is not. His action conforms to an implicit general judgment contrary to the true one.

How To Become Good

The reason Aristotle says that one does not become good by philosophizing and Aquinas that moral doctrine is of little or no value is that they are thinking of the aim of practical knowledge. When true moral knowledge fails to guide our choices, more and more general knowledge would not seem to be the remedy. The Greeks likened what is needed to the exercises in the gymnasium. One must school his appetite when lesser things are at issue if it is to be strong enough to follow true moral knowledge in more demanding situations. *Fasting allays concupiscence,* in the traditional phrase. If we mindlessly indulge ourselves in small things we will do so in great things as well; and if we deny ourselves in small things, this can affect our behavior when the stakes are high.

CHANGING ONE'S MIND/CHANGING ONE'S LIFE

One does not have to be morally good to acquire true moral knowledge at the level of generality, nor is he morally good by dint of having such knowledge. The passage from not-knowing to knowing alters our mind. But there is no automatic passage from such general knowledge to particular action because more than general knowledge is involved in action. Our choices bear on particulars seen as good. True moral knowledge is a necessary condition for changing our behavior from bad to good, but it is far from being sufficient.

Forgive me for rattling on about such matters, but there is method in my madness. What I have tested your patience by recalling is important for the question of this lecture but also for the next. In that I will examine the way in which both Kierkegaard and Newman seek to generalize Aristotle's account of practical discourse to cover all discourse, particularly that having to do with knowledge of God. But for the moment, what I have recalled enables me to address the misgiving I pointed out earlier. If a proof for the existence of God is a good one why does it not change the life of the one who accepts it?

A first reply to this is that such a demand cannot reasonably be made even of true moral knowledge that has as its aim to guide our choices. *A fortiori* it cannot be made of theoretical knowledge. Knowledge of God cannot be thought of as practical knowledge in terms of the account we have given earlier. It is theoretical knowledge through and through. The point of a proof of God's existence is to enable us to move from a state of not knowing to knowing a truth about the way things are. Thus it is mistaken to ask for an effect of such theoretical knowledge that we would not ask even of moral knowledge as it can be learned and taught.

And yet, as the much cited passage from Saint Paul more than suggests, the misbehavior of the pagan Romans was inexcusable because from the things that are made they could come to knowledge of the invisible things of God. When Augustine says that he would know but two things, God and the soul, he clearly sees such knowledge as relevant for life. The negative side of what Paul said to the Romans is the Dostoevskian dictum that if God does not exist, anything goes—as Cole Porter put it. Clearly theoretical truths have practical implications even though they are not as such principles or maxims to be realized in our choices. That God exists may not have any immediate "therefore" in the practical order, but knowing that God exists entails, in some sense of 'entails,' that our conduct should be of a certain kind.

So too, one who thought it true that there is nothing in man that survives death, that his animating principle, like that of dandelions and elephants, ceases to be when he as a person ceases to be, would doubtless be influenced by this belief in the way he organizes his life. If death is the end, not only our faith would be in vain, but perhaps much of our morals as well. There are of course good-hearted atheists and pleasant folk who think of themselves and others as ingenious computers but who nonetheless live exemplary lives. The question arises as to whether they could feel obliged to do so if their beliefs are true. Last October, I recalled what Jean-Paul Sartre said in *Existentialism Is a Humanism*. If God does not exist, we have no nature, there are no guidelines of choice antecedent to choice, we are free through and through.

But even on the contrary assumption—that there is a God, we have a nature, and this entails actions of a certain kind—our freedom must be engaged. This produces paradoxes, some of them amusing. Aristotle speaks of a man who had false general knowledge of what he ought to do, but lacking the courage of his convictions, acted contrary to his knowledge, and thus effectively did the right thing. Does flawed knowledge plus weakness of will equal good action? Surely not. But the flaw, like Huck Finn's acceptance of slavery as good, and acting contrary to this supposed truth, is at the level of general knowledge.

INTELLECTUS SPECULATIVUS EXTENSIONE FIT PRACTICUS

Those who accept the fact/value dichotomy as good money often argue that practical thinking is autonomous. Practical principles or norms cannot be *deduced* from theoretical statements about the way the world is or even about the way we are. This may seem to be merely a way of making the point behind our noting that it is wrong to expect a proof for God's existence to have immediate practical import. By speaking of deduction, we are invited to imagine an argument in which the premises are observations about the way things are and the conclusion is that we ought to do something. This is how Hume posed the problem.

But clearly the knowledge that God exists and that the human soul is immortal have practical import. The movement from such truths to judgments—at however high a level of generality—about what we ought to do is spoken of by Thomas Aquinas as an extension. How might we understand that?

If God exists and he has made us in order that we might enjoy eternal happiness with him, God is the ultimate end of human existence. As goodness itself and our ultimate good, God clearly has practical import for human beings. *You have made us for yourself, O Lord, and our hearts are restless until they rest in thee.* Any object of choice is a good, though not goodness. The formality of goodness under which any particular thing is chosen is our comprehensive good, our ultimate end. It is one thing to say that Guinness is good to taste and another to say that Guinness is good for you. If you were nothing but the capacity to taste, the two might be identical. But the pleasant objects of taste do not themselves exhaust even the things that willy-nilly excite our sense desire. The pursuit of any object is done on the implicit understanding that it is good for me to pursue it. And not just good for my taste; for me to satisfy my desire for Guinness here and now is judged to be good *for me.* The glutton seeks to make the satisfaction of taste the be-all and end-all of his life, as if anything else were good only insofar as it serves that end. *Cujus deus venter est,* as St. Paul says.

One must first know that God exists in order to see that he is our ultimate end, that is, the goodness we seek in any object of choice which is perforce a partial good, a participation in goodness. For that matter, there are traditional proofs of a first goodness or the ultimate final cause which is a proof of the existence of God. Nor is this a truth only available to religious believers. To suggest that (theoretically) true knowledge of that in which our good consists is not relevant to the discourse which ends in our doing something makes the distinction between theoretical and practical something other than two uses of a continuous act of reasoning.

Students of Aristotle have long been struck by the way in which the discussion of the human good in the *Nicomachean Ethics* terminates in an identification of our good with contemplation of the divine, Book X seeming to segue into Book Lambda of the *Metaphysics*. Aristotle is speaking of a good that is attainable in this life by our own efforts. But the *Ethics* sees *theoria* as the *telos* of moral action. And since it is not the task of moral philosophy to prove the existence of God, his existence must be presupposed by this account of our practical life. It may seem merely a feature of it as a common noun that 'good' can be predicated of any and every particular good. This alone does not prove that there is a good over and above particular goods. But 'good' as our *comprehensive* good is not predicable of any particular good. The way in which our over-all good controls particular choices is to make the *raison d'être* of any choice the judgment that it is good for me to choose this here and now. To identify the human comprehensive good with the object of contemplation was one of Aristotle's most daring and profound moves, and one that is often misunderstood.

When Aristotle says that the end of mind theoretical is truth and that of mind practical the good, he is not reifying these faculties as if they undertook their activities of themselves. Rather he is drawing attention to different purposes we can have in using our minds. The pursuit of truth is not an activity of some disembodied reason, but something we set out to do. It is a moral act, which must meet the standards of any other moral act. We choose to pursue the truth although what the truth is is not something we decide. The intellectual life is something flesh and blood human beings engage in, in particular settings, at definite times, for ulterior purposes, good and bad. The natural desire to know is not something we choose to have: it is a given. "All men by nature desire to know." The activities of our sense powers to some degree take place whether or not we wish. The desire for pleasure and the reflexive movement from the painful are not instinctive acts we choose to have. For reasons no pagan philosopher understood, we seem to be at war with ourselves. [They knew about the war, of course; it was Original Sin they were unaware of.] The life of a human being is a task in a way that the life of no other creature is. The rational direction of our various impulses and inclinations is the most fundamental and abiding instance of that task. The conscious and voluntary pursuit of objects to which we are naturally inclined involves the judgment that to pursue them here and now in these circumstances and in this way is a reasonable course of action, reasonable because such a pursuit contributes to our overall good.

This is as true of our natural desire for truth as it is of the object of any other natural inclination. There are morally good and bad ways of pursuing the truth and merely the successful achievement of the truth is not a sufficient moral warrant. A human being who pursued truth as if he were a pure spirit with no other obligations would be a morally defective human being.

ENVOI

The question as to the moral import of a successful proof of God's existence prompted us to recall the problematic relationship between even general moral knowledge and our actions. In the course of doing this, we nonetheless were able to respond to the import of the question, which is again supported by our favored Pauline passage. The discursive movement from theoretical knowledge—e.g., God's existence, the immortality of the soul—to action is analogous to the movement from general practical knowledge and action. The acting person is a unit, he has but one mind, and it is scarcely odd that, however formally different theoretical and practical knowing are, that a person perceives the relevance of the theoretical for the practical that permits, if he is virtuous, a smooth flow from both theoretical and general practical knowledge to this deed here and now.

But what if natural theology is rejected? How then can the mind relate to God? The existential or moral ambiance within which even abstract thinking must take place was something on which, in their various ways, the two men I shall discuss in my next lecture insisted. Both Kierkegaard and Newman discuss the human or existential setting in which we relate to God and check our tendency to think of ourselves as mere minds. But in doing so they put a remarkable premium on practical knowing.

FEBRUARY 10, 2000

Truth and Subjectivity

I have discussed the context within which a proof works, a context which is one of *doctrina* rather than *inventio*. We would not perhaps speak of someone proving something to himself, or if we did we would imagine him duplicated and occupying the roles of the one who addresses as well as that of addressee. Thomas Aquinas might thus read his Five Ways some time after having written them. In any case, we were concerned with the presuppositions of a proof considered as a text on the page functioning as a proof. The process of proving is complete when the addressee has reenacted in his own mind what the teacher had previously enacted in his. The teacher is the occasion of the thought process in his addressee and the proof as text is his instrument.

SUBJECTIVITY AFTER TRUTH

The upshot of the successful proving of a truth is that the learner has passed from not-knowing to knowing, from being able to know to actually knowing. This change in his mind has as its term the possession of a truth, that is, his mind has been brought into conformity with the way things are. But we have also seen that often, notably in the case of a proof of God's existence, much more than thinking differently than before is demanded of the proof. If such a proof were sound and someone accepted it, this acceptance should be manifested in his life. This diffi-culty arises either from asking too much of a proof or too little.

An austere response—we gave a version of it in the previous lec-ture—would be that once the distinction between changing one's mind and changing one's life is grasped, it is seen to be a confusion to ask that a proof should have so dramatic and existential an effect.

But this response can make one uneasy. Since proving involves thinking, it may seem to follow from this response that thinking has nothing to do with changing one's life. The realm of thought would be static, impersonal, inefficacious beyond the realm of mind; the realm of action would perhaps be delivered over to the passions, with reason op-erating as their slave if it got into the picture at all.

This led us on in the last lecture to a discussion of the difference be-tween the theoretical and practical uses of our mind. While the former seeks truth for its own sake, which is the perfection of thinking as such, when we use our mind practically we are seeking knowledge that can guide activities other than thinking, such as choosing. If the first ques-tion was, "Why does not theoretical knowledge have a practical effect?" it gave way to the far more agonizing question as to why practical knowledge often has no effect on our practice. This gap between knowl-edge and action would seem to be an essential defect in practical knowl-edge, whereas if theoretical truth influences action this would seem to be an incidental result of it.

In turning to the recurrent problem of the relation of knowledge to virtue, I sought to summarize Aristotle's teaching on the matter as supplemented by his disciple Thomas Aquinas. If one does not become good by philosophizing and if moral doctrine is of little or no value, as Aristotle and Thomas respectively said, the very difference between the-oretical and practical knowledge seems called into question. If both are mere instances of thought and neither has a predictable and as it were necessary effect on what the knower does, what good are they? More se-riously, if thought does not influence what we do, what does?

The discussion of these issues led us back to the difficulty posed to proofs for the existence of God. One can claim Pauline authority for the view that there is a connection between knowing that God exists and behavior in accord with that knowledge. Our suggestion here was that, *pace* those who take the fact/value split as dogma, the practical use of reason depends upon and grows out of its theoretical use. A successful proof of God's existence can lead on to the recognition that God is the ultimate end of the universe and more particularly of the moral agent. From such considerations, a morals that accords with the theoretical knowledge can develop.

But is it enough to say that certain practical consequences can derive from knowledge of God, with of course all the provisos about the way in which practical knowledge can fail to achieve its appointed end? This might be called the *Subjectivity after Truth* position. Two of the most formidable minds of the nineteenth century, Søren Kierkegaard and John Henry Newman, seem to require far more of us. For these two, though in different ways, subjectivity becomes the very possibility of truth, and both will define subjectivity in terms of the culminating judgment of what Aristotle called the practical syllogism.

SUBJECTIVITY IS THE TRUTH

I have had occasion before in these lectures to draw upon the thought of Kierkegaard. We found it necessary to reject his suggestion that there can be no proof of God's existence because you cannot prove the existence of anything. But it would be misleading in the extreme to portray Kierkegaard—or his designated spokesman in matters philosophical, Johannes Climacus—as wanting to get involved in a discussion of classical proofs. Kierkegaard wants to sweep them off the table as irrelevant, misleading, and distracting from the one thing needful.

When Climacus in *The Concluding Unscientific Postscript to the Philosophical Fragments* turns to the question of truth, the discussion begins in what looks to be a standard way.[1] Whether we take the correspondence theory or the idealist theory of truth, it involves two *relata*, thought and being. As for the former, if truth is thought's conformity to being, and being is taken to be the changing things of this world, then thought aims at a moving target and can achieve only an approximation. As for the idealist theory, if truth is the identity of thought and being it seems only an "abstract self-identity."

---

1. Søren Kierkegaard, *Concluding Unscientific Postscript*, trans. David F. Swenson and Walter Lowrie (Princeton, N.J.: Princeton University Press, 1941). Chapter II of Part Two is the relevant text: pp. 169–224.

Abstract thought may continue as long as it likes to rewrite this thought in varying phraseology, it will never get any farther. As soon as the being which corresponds to the truth comes to be empirically concrete, the truth is put in process of becoming, and is again by way of anticipation the conformity of thought with being. This conformity is actually realized for God, but it is not realized for any existing spirit, who is himself existentially in process of becoming. (170)

It is the existing subject, the knower as a man of flesh and blood, to whom Kierkegaard would direct our attention, and that is to direct it away from "objective reflection" which points away from the subject. "For a subjective reflection the truth becomes a matter of appropriation, of inwardness, of subjectivity, and thought must probe more and more deeply into the subject and his subjectivity" (171).

Whatever one makes of his remarks about objective truth, it is clear that Kierkegaard is interested in practical knowledge and the truth appropriate to it. One seeks to appropriate, to become, what one knows, and this requires that the knowledge be assimilable in this manner. If the human subject is incidental to objective thought, the very reverse is true of subjective thinking. Knowledge that bears an essential relation to the subject is the only kind of thinking Climacus will regard as essential. "Only ethical and ethico-religious knowledge has an essential relationship to the existence of the knower" (177). The definition of truth appropriate to this emphasis is this: "*An objective uncertainty held fast in an appropriation process of the most passionate inwardness is the truth*, the highest truth attainable for an *existing* individual" (182). That Kierkegaard is speaking of practical knowledge as opposed to theoretical in the Aristotelian sense is clear from his invocation of Aristotle for this distinction.[2] That there is an undeniable animus against abstract or theoretical thought should not detract us from the main point. "The real subject is not the cognitive subject, since in knowing he moves in the sphere of the possible; the real subject is the ethically existing subject" (281).

But it would be untrue to the Kierkegaardian effort to see it as simply a preference for the practical over the theoretical. The role

2. He cites *De anima* III, 10 on p. 278, and identifies what he has been calling subjective thought with practical thinking in the Aristotelian sense.

assigned Climacus in the literature is to lead the reader *"Away from speculation!"*[3] toward a correct understanding of what it means to be a Christian. *Understanding* here must mean the existential understanding captured by the notion of subjective thought. The Christian task is to become like Christ, to assimilate the Gospel message into one's life. Kierkegaard, and Climacus, are annoyed by the attempt to turn Christianity into a mere occasion for scholarship and are ruthless with those who do.

We have earlier seen the way in which Kierkegaard has Climacus dismiss the whole project of natural theology. And it is precisely our knowledge of God that forms the prelude to the definition of existential truth.[4] Any attempt to attain objective knowledge of God becomes an endless approximation process that can never achieve its term. This dismissal echoes the viewpoint of the *Fragments*. The only way God can be attained is subjectively.

> The existing individual who chooses to pursue the subjective way apprehends instantly the entire dialectical difficulty involved in having to use some time, perhaps a long time, in finding God objectively; and he feels this dialectical difficulty in all its painfulness, because every moment is wasted in which he does not have God. That very instant he has God, not by virtue of any objective deliberation, but by virtue of the infinite passion of inwardness. (179)

A second discussion preliminary to the definition of subjective truth is the question of the immortality of the soul. The objective proofs are taken to be inconclusive or wrongheaded. The matter is settled subjectively.

I will take this as sufficient basis for the claim that Kierkegaard generalizes what is peculiar to the practical order and wants it to encompass what had hitherto been taken to be questions that had an objective solution, viz. God's existence and the immortality of the soul. It is not simply that he opts for the practical as opposed to the theoretical. He absorbs the whole range of issues that had belonged to natural theology

---

3. Kierkegaard, *The Point of View*, trans. Walter Lowrie (New York: Oxford University Press, 1950), 75.

4. "Let us take as an example the knowledge of God" (ibid., 178 ff.).

into the practical or subjective order. The truth that God exists is established by living as if he existed.[5]

THE ILLATIVE SENSE

John Henry Newman tells us that in his discussion of what he calls the illative sense he, like Bishop Butler, is not interested in metaphysics but has a practical aim. But he differs from Butler in this that he wishes to go beyond mere probability to the mind's certainty about the truth of things. The illative sense is presented as the perfection or virtue of the ratiocinative faculty of the mind.[6] For all that, Newman regards as given a human nature which differs from others in that "though man cannot change what he is born with, he is a being of progress with relation to his perfection and characteristic good" (274). But nature as given is inchoate and rudimentary and must be brought to perfection.

Inference and assent are the instruments of acquiring this perfection. The ultimate object of this quest is God, but it has pleased God to make the route to him circuitous and rugged above all other investigations. The judging and reasoning that will take us to him are perfected by the illative sense.[7] It is at this point that Newman relates what he is saying to Aristotle, noting that Aristotle called "the faculty"—he must mean the virtue—which guides judgment in matters of conduct *phronesis*. An ethical system supplies laws, general rules, guiding principles, but the application of these to the particular is the task of *phronesis*. Is Newman merely citing the counterpart in the practical order of what he has been discussing in the theoretical?

5. "In this manner God certainly becomes a postulate, but not in the otiose manner in which the word is commonly understood. It becomes clear rather that the only way in which an existing individual comes into relation with God, is when the dialectical contradiction brings his passion to the point of despair, and helps him to embrace God with the 'category of despair' (faith). Then the postulate is so far from being arbitrary that it is precisely a life-necessity. It is then not so much that God is a postulate, as that the existing individual's postulation of God is a necessity" (ibid., 179, note).

6. John Henry Newman, *An Essay in Aid of a Grammar of Assent* (Notre Dame, Ind.: University of Notre Dame Press, 1979), 271.

7. "It is the mind that reasons, and that controls its own reasonings, not any technical apparatus of words and propositions. This power of judging and concluding, when in its perfection, I call the Illative Sense" (ibid., 276).

Though Aristotle, in his *Nicomachean Ethics*, speaks of φρόνησις (as the virtue of the δοξαστικον generally, and as being concerned generally with contingent matter (vi.4), or what I have called the concrete and of its function being, as regards that matter, ἀληθεύειν τῷ καταφάναι η ἀποφάναι (ibid. 3), he does not treat of it in that work in its general relation to truth and the affirmation of truth, but only as it bears upon τα πρακτα.[8]

Newman goes on for several pages giving an account of Aristotelian *phronesis*. He describes it as the controlling principle in inferences, and suggests that there are as many kinds of *phronesis* as there are virtues. That he does indeed intend to extend *phronesis* beyond the practical order is clear enough. The illative sense is taken to be one and the same in all concrete matters. "We do not reason in one way in chemistry or law, in another in morals and religion; but in reasoning on any subject whatever, which is concrete, we proceed, as far as indeed as we can, by the logic of the language, but we are obliged to supplement it by the more subtle and elastic logic of thought; for forms by themselves prove nothing" (281).[9]

I take such passages to mean that what Aristotle called *phronesis*, which he confined to the practical order, can be extended to all reasoning on concrete matters. The Illative Sense is the name of this virtue which is the perfection of reasoning on whatever concrete object it may be operating. Newman explicitly gathers the reasoning that leads to knowledge of God's existence under this umbrella.

A NEGATIVE REACTION

While Kierkegaard may be said to be skeptical about the objective or theoretical approach to God and to prefer the subjective, since subjective thinking is the mode of access to God and since subjective thinking is exemplified by practical reasoning, it is reasonable to assume that the criteria for truth in practical reasoning are the criteria for subjective

8. Ibid., 277, note 1.
9. ". . . in no class of concrete reasonings, whether in experimental science, historical research, or theology, is there any ultimate test of truth and error in our inferences besides the trustworthiness of the Illative Sense that gives its sanction" (ibid., 281).

truth in the Kierkegaardian sense. As for Newman, he is even more explicit in generalizing the virtue that Aristotle called the perfection of practical thinking, *phronesis* or prudence. What is to be made of this?

Aristotle distinguishes the truth of judgments in the theoretical order from those in the practical order. In the former, truth is the mind's conformity to what is. Such conformity requires fixity and bears on the essential rather than the incidental in changeable things. The singular changeable things in the world cannot as such be proper objects of knowledge in the strong sense, of judgments whose truth escapes the ravages of change and accident. This is what led Plato to posit Forms or Ideas, of which we are only reminded by sensible things and which are the fitting objects of knowledge. Aristotle can be said to locate the forms in the singulars so that the *kind* of changeable things can be abstracted and grasped by the mind and provide a kind of necessity that its singular instances lack. But in practical knowing, where knowledge aims to guide singular contingent actions in the here and now, such truth cannot be had. So it is that Aristotle speaks of practical truth, the truth of the proximate judgment that is embedded in this action.

Thomas Aquinas, in discussing practical truth, contrasts it to speculative or theoretical truth by saying that the judgment of theoretical mind is true when in conformity with the way things are, whereas the truth of the practical judgment involved in a singular action comes about by its conformity with rectified appetite. That is, unless the appetite has been schooled by moral virtue to the true end of man, a correct judgment as to what a virtue demands here and now cannot be made, or made only with enormous difficulty, as in the case of the one Aristotle calls continent. If appetite is not perfected by virtue, perfect or imperfect, the appetite will draw a person toward the good it habitually pursues. That is, a true judgment of what I am to do in these contingent particular circumstances is guaranteed by the fact that my will is fixed on the true good. It is the just man who can judge truly the demands of justice in this instance.

One could go on. Taken as developed by Aristotle and Aquinas, there seems to be no way in which the existence of God and the immortality of soul could be the object of true judgments of practical reason. Any effort to generalize practical reason over the whole range of reasoning would seem consequently to be wrongheaded. In the case of the existence of God, it could be made to seem as if, having thought and argued to a certain point, one simply asserts that God exists. Of course to suggest that either Kierkegaard or Newman would hold such a position as baldly stated as this would be libelous. So having given a negative judgment on their effort taken literally, I shall now go on to see how it might be benignly understood.

A Positive Critique

Kierkegaard and Newman are not alone in wanting to expand the classical discussion of practical reasoning to cover what it was not classically taken to cover. Jacques Maritain was greatly impressed by a distinction between two kinds of wisdom based on two kinds of judgment that is made early in the *Summa theologiae* when it is asked whether sacred science is a wisdom. Wisdom is manifested in wise judgments. Thomas contrasts a judgment *per modum cognitionis* with what he calls a judgment *per modum inclinationis*. The latter is also sometimes called a judgment *per modum connaturalitatis* and it is under this name that Maritain sought to expand its applicability beyond the range assigned it by Aquinas.

... cum iudicium ad sapientem pertineat, secundum duplicem modum iudicandi dupliciter sapientia accipitur. Contingit enim aliquem iudicare uno modo per modum inclinationis: sicut qui habet habitum virtutis, recte iudicat de his quae secundum virtutem agenda, inquantum ad illa inclinatur: unde in X Ethic. dicitur quod virtuosus est mensura et regula actuum humanorum. Alio modo per modum cognitionis, sicut aliquis instructus in scientia morali, posset iudicare de actibus virtutus, etiam si virtutem non haberet.
(*ST* 1.1.7.*ad* 3*m*)

Since judgment pertains to wisdom, there are two kinds of wisdom insofar as there are two kinds of judgment. For it happens that someone judges in one way by way of inclination, as one who has the habit of a virtue judges rightly about the things to be done according to that virtue, insofar as he is inclined to them. Thus in *Ethics* 10 the virtuous person is said to be the rule and measure of human acts. In another way, by way of knowledge, as someone instructed in moral science can judge of the acts of virtue even if he does not have that virtue.

In the text, Thomas is contrasting a general judgment about a moral matter, one that might be made by a moral philosopher or theologian, with the judgment about a certain kind of practical matter made by the virtuous person. Of course he is not suggesting that moral philosophers are not virtuous persons—then again he is not suggesting that they are—rather he is pointing out that a judgment on a level of generality, about a type of act, is not dependent on the appetitive condition of the judge. On the other hand, the virtuous person's judgment as such depends, as we have seen, on his appetite being perfected by moral virtue. If he were asked for advice, he can give a judgment based, not on generalities, but on his inclination to or connaturality with the good.

Maritain suggested that poetic knowledge, the knowledge that is presupposed by the technical knowledge that goes into the construction of a poem, can be regarded as connatural knowledge. This development of Maritain's is fascinating in itself and deserves attention, but I mention it now simply as another example of someone seeking to apply the characteristics of the judgment of prudence to other areas.[10]

But there is another expansion and one far more relevant to what Kierkegaard and Newman do that is suggested by the text and that Maritain also noticed and emphasized in a number of places. Although Thomas's first example of the judgment by way of inclination is a particular moral judgment, where wisdom would mean the practical wisdom signified by *phronesis*, he also illustrates it by the Gift of Wisdom, which is to be distinguished as well from the wisdom exemplified in theological treatises.

Primus igitur modus iudicandi de rebus divinis, pertinet ad sapientiam quae ponitur donum Spiritus Sancti, secundum illud 1 Cor. 2, 15: *spiritualis homo iudicat omnia, etc.* et Dionysius dicit 2 cap. *De divinis nominibus: Hierotheus doctus est non solum discens, sed et patiens divina.* Secundus autem modus iudicandi pertinet ad hanc doctrinam, secundum quod per studium habetur; licet eius principia ex revelatione habeantur. (*ST* 1.1.6.*ad* 3*m*)	The first way of judging about divine things pertains to the wisdom which is a gift of the Holy Spirit, according to 1 Cor. 2:15: 'The spiritual man judges all things. . .'" And Denis says in *On the divine names*, chap. 2, "Hierotheus is learned not only by studying but also by experiencing divine things." The second way of judging pertains to this doctrine, insofar as it is acquired by study, though its principles are had by way of revelation.

10. See Chapters 10 and 11 in my *Art and Prudence: Studies in the Thought of Jacques Maritain* (Notre Dame, Ind.: University of Notre Dame Press, 1988).

In the passage at issue then, Thomas is suggesting the following analogy: As a judgment in moral science is to the judgment of the prudent man, so judgments about divine things in theology are to the judgments one makes according to the gift of the Holy Spirit. The latter is an experiential judgment. Thus, there is knowledge of divine things that can be compared to the particular moral judgment. However, this knowledge is due to an infused gift which is the prerogative of the Christian believer and thus would be consequent on certainty that there is a God rather than productive of it. Is there any way in which the Aristotelian notion of practical knowledge in particular could be applied to theoretical knowledge of God and of the immortality of the soul?

As Newman's *Apologia pro vita sua* makes clear, when confronted with a demand to give the objective reasons for his religious conversion, he replied in effect that that is not how profound changes in one's life take place, that is, simply as a result of argument. There were of course arguments along the way but in their regard Newman speaks of a convergence of probabilities. This seems to mean both that the arguments are not conclusive or probative *and* that they, taken singly and perhaps all together, are insufficient to explain what he decided to do. Since Newman is discussing a movement *within* religious faith, the passage from being a Christian in one sense (an Anglican) to being a Christian in another (a Roman Catholic), the discussion takes place on a level that is not immediately helpful to natural theology. So too, since Kierkegaard does not think proofs for God's existence are conclusive, he can be taken to be speaking of how it is that *belief* in the sense of religious faith comes about. It is not, he insists, a necessary conclusion of a demonstration. The conclusion involved would be something like *credo in deum*, so neither can this be of any immediate help in discussing natural theology.

A MODEST PROPOSAL

One of the attractions of the *Grammar of Assent* lies in its emphasis on the fact that reasoning and arguing and concluding are things that concrete individuals do. Not only is the cognitive process by which I arrived at knowledge of God by way of a proof something that *I* do, *my* act of reasoning, it is also a moral act and thus finds its native habitat in the subjectivity of the thinker. Kierkegaard observed that objective thought points away from the subject, and so it does. Let us assume, contrary to Climacus, that there are sound arguments for the existence of God and that these are exercises of theoretical reasoning. While such arguments have to be made by some individual person, that person is not thematic to the argument, not what the argument is about. Nonetheless, the argument can be appraised from two points of view, intrinsically, let us say, and morally.

Intrinsically, the argument will be appraised in terms of logic and of the truth of the propositions which enter into it. If it passes these appraisals, it can be accounted a good argument and the reasoning to have succeeded. But, since the objective truth was attained by the singular acts of reasoning of an individual person, what he has done can also be appraised in moral terms. That is, was his devoting himself to this speculation at this time and place, in these circumstances, good or not? It is conceivable that a good and successful piece of reasoning will get bad moral marks because of the circumstances in which the person engaged in it. Let us imagine a natural theologian whose learning has been gained from books he has stolen; let us imagine, more proximately, that as he labors at his desk, he is ignoring his wife and children and perhaps his own health as well. Perhaps he has plugged his computer into a neighbor's socket and is working on purloined electricity. And so on. Such circumstances might lead us to say of what he was up to in his study that he was acting badly.

Of course, the intrinsic and moral appraisals of reasoning are incidental to one another. One who acts in an exemplary way in pursuing a proof of God's existence can nonetheless fail to achieve the result he is after, or achieve one that is flawed logically. Here we will criticize his argument but not condemn his behavior. Do these elementary considerations cast any light on the relationship between subjectivity and natural theology?

Let me advert to considerations in my first set of lectures to suggest a positive answer to that question. In discussing the question of Christian philosophy and the charge that the believer cannot engage sincerely in philosophy because he is already certain on the basis of his faith of many of the things that come up for discussion in philosophy, I granted the description of the believing philosopher, but not the supposed consequence. To do so would be to disqualify anyone from engaging in philosophy. The antecedent beliefs of the Christian are easy to identify and label, but *everyone* comes to philosophy with a set of antecedent beliefs. Far from entailing that all arguments are merely bad reasons for what one already holds, I suggested that there is an objective appraisal—I have been calling it an intrinsic appraisal tonight—of arguments that is independent of the antecedent dispositions of its framer, whatever they might be.

Now the upshot of that seems to be to acknowledge but deem irrelevant antecedent beliefs of any kind. That was not my conclusion, for reasons I will not repeat: I think Christian faith is of inestimable help in achieving the ends of philosophizing. This is nowhere more evident than when it is a question of asking what reasons could be given to show that God exists.

One who comes to philosophizing with materialist presumptions, with an animus against metaphysics and skepticism about the existence of God, is in a bad subjective condition to undertake the philosophical task. Consider. If God exists this is a truth of paramount importance. Anyone must agree that failure to acknowledge the one on whom the universe and all in it depend is not a minor defect. One would be out of tune with the reality of which he is a part. Prior to undertaking the task of natural theology it is well for us to have a sense of the seriousness of that undertaking. This does not guarantee success of course, but a successful outcome is viewed as a possibility. A negative antecedent attitude all but guarantees that the task will not be undertaken in a way that will allow the truth of the matter to shine through.

Subjectivity is not the immediate source of objective truth, but there is a kind of subjective disposition that is open to objective truth and another that is closed even to its possibility.

Neither my negative nor my positive assessment of subjective or practical truth provides support for the generalization that both Kierkegaard and Newman want to make, each in his own way. By citing Aristotle, they invite an appraisal from one who, like Thomas Aquinas, stands within the Aristotelian tradition. For all that, speaking specifically of divine faith, there is good reason to liken its truth to practical truth. The concrete practical judgment is true when it is in conformity with a fixed and habitual appetitive orientation to the true good. Faith is a habit of speculative intellect, a virtue which enables one to judge well and truly of divine things. Of course any intellectual virtue perfects mental activity. Science is a virtue which enables the one having it to judge well and truly of a certain subject matter, but the truth of such judgments lies in their conformity with the way things are. In the case of faith, its objects remain incomprehensible to the mind of the believer. It cannot be the evidence of the object then which explains his judgment of divine things. The assent of faith is given accordingly because of an impetus of the will moved by grace, something captured by Augustine in the phrase *Nemo credit nisi volens*. This essential dependence of faith on will's desire for happiness for the truth of its judgments causes Thomas to say that faith is more akin to virtue in the obvious sense, moral virtue, than are such intellectual habits as science and art. Insofar as Kierkegaard and Newman can be taken to be speaking of divine faith, then, calling it subjective truth puts them in the same neighborhood as Thomas Aquinas. In the case of Kierkegaard, since the only access to God is by way of faith, this serves to support his pseudonym's claim that truth is subjectivity. It is more difficult in the case of Newman to arrive at this irenic conclusion, because he wants the illative sense, that is, prudence, to range over all subject matters, theoretical and practical. This can only be accommodated in the way indicated above, the way characterized as benign.

FEBRUARY 15, 2000

That God Exists

M y lectures seem always to be removing impediments on the path to natural theology, as if, against my philosophical bent, I were establishing the conditions of the possibility of natural theology. That continues to be the case tonight when I turn at last to the *via manifestior*, the proof of God's existence from motion.

A Proximate Obstacle

The conclusion of the proof of God's existence drawn from motion depends upon the truth of the premises. Since those premises are not self-evident, they in turn must be proved. As it happens, the proof, which can be simply stated in terms of three propositions, depends for its intelligibility on a vast number of analyses, definitions, and arguments that have preceded its formulation. In the *Summa theologiae*, as I have observed, we are given brief statements meant to recall the philosophical knowledge already possessed by those beginning the study of theology. They are expected to recall the proof from motion that is found in Books 7 and 8 of Aristotle's *Physics* and reposes on what has been established in the previous books.

This reminder brings to the fore the most obvious difficulty that you and I, living at the beginning of the third millennium, must have with this proof: Aristotle's *Physics*. If Aristotelian natural philosophy is the basis for the soundness of the proof from motion the claim must seem incredible. How, save in some Pickwickian sense, could anything of the natural science of the fourth century B.C. be said to be true? We have been schooled to think that the advances in natural science that came about with Copernicus and Galileo, with Newton, with Einstein, et al., have rendered such primitive efforts obsolete. Indeed, to call them obsolete might seem to concede too much, as if at one time Aristotelian natural science explained anything about the world.

When this difficulty is made explicit, we realize that it is part of the implicit intellectual atmosphere in which we all have been raised. Since none of us could possibly be immune to such an attitude toward the Greek science of the fourth century B.C., the problem must be confronted at the outset, on pain of making any subsequent discussion of merely historical interest. Perhaps anyone would agree that, if we conceded what Aristotle means by 'motion,' 'moving,' and 'being moved', and by the impossibility of an infinite series of moved movers, then of course it would follow that there must be a first unmoved mover. But haven't all these assumptions been consigned to the dustbin of the history of science?

The World of Experience

That things are not always what they seem is the delight of infancy, the consolation of childhood, and a matter of dwindling hope as one grows older. But this received opinion about the past is put to strange purposes when a young person takes an introductory course in philosophy. It is not unusual for philosophers to see their task as disabusing their beginning students of the beliefs they bring with them to the classroom. The assumption is that these young minds are riddled with confusions derived from a multiplicity of sources but that now, finally, thanks to what we call Philosophy 101 in my country, these students are going to have their minds cleansed of confusion.

Not an ignoble aim, of course, provided the confusion is on the student side of the lectern. Your senses sometimes deceive you. So do mine. What can be done about this? One of the first things we learn to do is to correct for such mistakes. The way to do so is usually fairly straightforward. The distance from us of an object, its color, its shape—

when we are mistaken about these, we correct the mistake not by taking leave of our senses but by appealing to them. In the *Protagoras*, Plato
says things about the art of perspective before proposing an analogy of
it in moral matters. Water distorted my vision and I thought the stick
was crooked, but *voilà!* Here it is, straight as a stick. The senses are self-
correcting in the sense that the person whose senses they are can make
the kind of appeal just alluded to.

But some philosophers move from the undeniable fact that our
senses sometimes deceive us to the conclusion that we can never trust
the judgments we make on the basis of them, because for all we know
our senses are deceiving us right now. Just to be on the safe side, then,
we should set aside all reliance on the senses. But this is somewhat like
swearing off food because we sometimes get an upset stomach. More
significantly, it sometimes sends people in pursuit of some apriori jus-
tification for trusting their senses.

Early in the history of philosophy the distinction between appearance and reality was introduced in a marked way by Parmenides.
Reliance on our senses collided with the principle of coherence. If there
really was a world in which there are many things that are always changing, then, Parmenides announced, being would have to be not-being
and vice versa. Since that is untenable, he bade adieu to the world as
grasped by the senses, calling it mere appearance. In reality there is only
Being, period. Oddly enough, but significantly, Parmenides went on to
give an account of the many changing things in the world much as his
maligned predecessors had done. He called this the Way of Seeming and
he clearly could not get along without it. Presumably, it is in the world
of seeming that he and we and his book exist.

Inconsistency is the tribute that confusion pays to reality. When
Descartes is taking us through methodic doubt to the *cogito* he apparently forgets, and we perhaps do not notice, that in order to engage in
such ferocious doubting, we have to see the words before us, turn pages,
know French or Latin or translations thereof, and have acquaintance
with the things all those words mean. The Wizard of Oz created decep-
tive experience much as Descartes feigned to doubt everything.

We get the world back from Descartes, but is it the world we were
familiar with before we doubted it away? Colors are no more in bod-
ies than pain is in the knife. All kinds of sensible properties are made
merely subjective because it is only what is amenable to measurement

that has objectivity. But then how do we measure? How do we see the ruler or read the dials? This takes me to my second point.

WHAT DOES
SCIENCE EXPLAIN?

Such explanations of the things around us can seem to explain them away, as colors and secondary qualities are explained away early on in the scientific revolution. All that is left of them is their quantitative base. Thus the restored world, after the drama of methodic doubt, is not quite the world that was doubted away. This raises the question as to what the relationship is between the world of common experience and the scientific explanation of it.

In thinking about advances in the sciences we are likely to refer to the confusions of previous times which have been overcome thanks to progress in knowledge. There are myths as well, of course, such as that prior to Columbus people did not think of the world as round. There are accounts of early beliefs in the supposed magical or medicinal properties of things which have been set aside thanks to science. There is the suggestion—less often the outright claim—that the world of common sense and ordinary experience is destined to give way *in its entirety* to a scientific account. There is a fairly flat-footed way of addressing this suggestion.

Arthur Eddington, in a famous passage, asked what the relationship was between the table he was writing on and that table as he would explain it in terms of physics.[1] There was a dramatic contrast between them, almost as dramatic as the two tables of Pythagoras. His writing table had a solid surface which resisted the pressure of his hand upon it; its dimensions were fixed. If asked to give the size of his desk, he would answer the same today as he did yesterday. His desk was where it was and not somewhere else: it stood still. But when Eddington turned to a scientific account of that same table it seemed to dissolve immediately into a porous thing, a swarm of electrons, whose shape and posi-

---

1. Arthur Eddington, *The Nature of the Physical World* (New York: Macmillan, 1928).

tion were constantly altering. The solid everyday table evanesced in this analysis. Which account of the table is the right one?

I am addressing, then, the suggestion that the everyday account of the table is mistaken and corrigible, and that what corrects it is the scientific account of the real table. And it does so by wholly replacing it. Why is this nonsense? If the ordinary table is taken away there is nothing for the scientific account to account for. The world into which we were born and in which we grew up is not so much doubted away as explained away. The defensible view is that scientific explanations begin by accounting for the things of our ordinary experience.

Pre-scientific Knowledge?

It will be said that I am speaking of pre-scientific knowledge, as indeed I am. But I am concerned with the suggestion that all our knowledge of the world before we undertake the study of physics is wrong and must give way to the true account of physics—or to the truth that the development in physics is converging upon. And I have suggested that this would deprive the scientific explanation of having anything to explain. Reducing things to measurable properties enables us to gain a good deal of control over them but this is to give an exiguous account of the things that are.

What I shall mean by pre-scientific knowledge is the kind of knowledge about the world that scientists as well as ordinary folk live in, about which they know things that are true and which is presupposed by the scientific account but not replaced by it.

If it is the case that Eddington's ordinary knowledge of the world is presupposed by and not denied by his work as a physicist, it is also the case that truths about the world gained before the rise of science in our sense are not fourth-century B.C. truths, but simply truths about the world.

This is not of course to endorse the whole panoply of Aristotelian natural science. His astronomy has gone into the black hole reserved for discarded accounts. Perhaps even most of his natural science retains only historical interest. But is it plausible that everything he had to say about the natural world is false?

PROGRESS IN KNOWLEDGE OF NATURE

At the outset of his *Physics* Aristotle likens progress in our knowledge of nature to first seeing an object far off, knowing that there is something there, and, as it approaches us, gradually seeing that the something is alive, is human, is a male, is Albert Einstein. Our knowledge from being obscure becomes progressively less obscure and more distinct. Taking his cue from this, Aristotle offered the generalization that it is the nature of our knowledge that it begins with generic truths and seeks ever more specific knowledge of the thing first known generically. This is the reason why he begins as he does.

Are there certain truths, general though they would necessarily be, that cover all the things in nature, that is, all the things that come to be? The *Physics* is that first exploration.

After he reviews what his predecessors had to say about nature, much of it seemingly fantastic and falling somewhere between myth and explanation, Aristotle asks what, despite the wild diversity of views, his predecessors agreed on. There are agreements, he suggests, despite the undeniable diversity. All the accounts he has reviewed speak of change as involving something subject to contrary states. Change occurs when the subject loses one state and gains its contrary.

Is this true? Maybe. That is all he seeks to derive from this distillation of underlying assumptions. A probability. He then undertakes his own analysis of that which has come to be as the result of a change. You see before you someone who has acquired a profound and lasting admiration for that analysis. It seems to me quintessentially Aristotelian. In seeking to say something about all natural things, Aristotle must begin with an example that can be taken to stand for them all. He proposes that we ask what is involved when we say that a man becomes musical.

It is tempting to review that marvelous analysis here. You all know the upshot of it. Any change involves a subject that takes on a characteristic it previously lacked. Thanks to another example—whittling wood—these three elements are called matter (ὑλή), form (μόρφη), and privation (στερησις). These principles of change will be extended to changes of quantity and place as well as quality. And of the product of change it can consequently be said that it is a composite of matter and form. It is when Aristotle asks whether the subject of such changes can itself come into being that, on an analogy with the subject of incidental changes, he will call the subject of the change whereby a substance itself comes into being prime matter.

What is to be made of this analysis? It enables us to enunciate the truth that anything that comes to be as the result of a change is composed of matter and form. Since this is the first, the least, the most general thing that can be said about a natural thing, it would be wrong to regard it as profound. As general, it can be endlessly specified, and that is the task of the subsequent works Aristotle devoted to the things of nature. Within the *Physics* itself we find discussions of kinds of cause and of chance events, of motion, time, place. And eventually we find the proof that is our subject tonight.

This analysis may be called pre-scientific knowledge, if by science we mean a quantitative account, but it is surely not without a clarity and precision that goes beyond the ability to speak Greek. It represents a cognitive gain, however modest. And it is true. Our retrospective problem is not that it is false, but that it discusses change so differently than our physics. In much the same way we do not know what to make of Aristotle's definition of motion, since our laws of motion simply bypass such a task.

The Proof from Motion

Aristotle's definition of motion, as you know, is *the act of a being in potency insofar as it is in potency.* We might call it *the actualizing of a potency* but that could seem to introduce a synonym of the definiendum into the definition. Aristotle's definition is fine just as it is. Motion belongs to the thing moving, but it turns out that for it to move is for it to be moved. The seven ball at rest on the table could be in one of the pockets but the possibility will only become actual if something moves it, actualizes that potency. The pool ball cannot do it itself. Moving things are moved things. Could the universe be made up only of moved movers? That is the question that leads Aristotle to argue that there must be a first unmoved mover if there are to be any moved movers, if there is to be the whole set of moved movers.

Obviously the proof from motion has to be understood in its own terms and, I suggest, when it is, the proof clearly works. (Obviously this is a promissory note which invites objections and indeed expects them.) Say I am right in this. What reactions can be expected?

Impatience, first of all. It is difficult for us to imagine that things said about the natural world so long ago have stood the test of time. We are too used to the notion that all that has been superseded.

Sometimes, benevolent misunderstanding. One seeks to understand the proof without grasping the meaning Aristotle assigned to the terms and to the propositions.

NOT A HISTORICAL MATTER

Of course, if I am right, the fact that this proof was formulated in the fourth century B.C., and by Aristotle, is incidental to it. Anyone can reenact the thinking of the *Physics* and decide whether the analyses, definitions, and proofs make sense. Any comparison with contemporary physics should be postponed. This is not merely to put off the evil day, but to locate what Aristotle is doing relative to contemporary science.

If it is true, as I have suggested, that the scientist lives his life in a world knowable by him in a way that is prior to and presupposed by what he says about that world as scientist, we have an arena in which such analyses as Aristotle's fall. If we call them pre-scientific, this must not be taken to mean that they are destined to be superseded by a scientific analysis. Just as the things Eddington says about the table in his study are true and are not rivals of what he says about it from the viewpoint of mathematical physics, so the analyses of the *Physics* can be true without being rivals of science as it has come to be.[2] Surely no one would want to adopt the view that he knows no truths about the natural world save those that he learns from science. He couldn't learn those truths if that were true.

SO WHAT?

An advantage of having said even these few things about the most famous proof of God's existence is that earlier considerations may now

2. This analogy suggests itself: as Eddington's ordinary table is to the scientific account of the table, so the philosophy of nature is to natural science.

make more sense. That there is a first unmoved mover that moves all the moved movers may not set every pulse racing. It can seem terribly remote from our ordinary lives, it may seem not to make any difference. That is the dissatisfaction that Kierkegaard addressed—at least in part; I do not mean to reduce his literary effort to this—and Newman as well. How does such reasoning relate to the anguish with which we sometimes wonder whether there really is a God?

One of the merits of Newman's *Grammar* is that it relates the proof to the one proving, reminding us that so to dispose of one's time is a moral act. But who will not feel the force of Pascal's contrast of the God of the philosophers and the God of Abraham and Isaac? It may be worthwhile to ponder that contrast.

First of all, it goes without saying that, for a believer the theology of the philosopher is going to seem a poor thing. Absent is the whole context of sin and redemption and longing for God.

Second, Kierkegaard is right that when a believer sees the object of his faith simply as an occasion for speculation and learning, he is in a confused condition. And the proof of the prime mover is clearly an exercise in theoretical thinking.

But when Greek philosophy is looked at, not through the lens of Christianity, but in itself, the picture alters somewhat. The whole philosophical undertaking is meant to assuage a desire to understand that is not confined to theoretical matters. Furthermore, to stay with Aristotle, we have had occasion to note the way in which the theoretical wisdom of metaphysics becomes the object of the contemplation which is the fullest perfection of the kind of entity we are. There may be little unction in Aristotle, perhaps a Macedonian reticence, but the notion of philosophy as a way of life is as strong with him as it is with Plato.

Shortcuts

Anselm's proof in the *Proslogion* was prompted by the request that he come up with a shorter form of the proof he had advanced in the *Monologion*. The so-called Ontological Proof sought to make the denial of God's existence a logical absurdity.

Pascal's Wager is another effort to make short shrift of the question. If one lives his life as if God exists, and he does, things will go well in the next world; however, if one lives his life as if God does not exist, and he does, things will not go well in the next life. If one lives one's life as if God exists, and he does not, there will be no next life in which you could regret your choice. So there is only one way to lose: living as if God does not exist. Best to put one's money, and one's life, on the assumption that God exists.[3]

Not a very edifying approach to the question. Pascal himself seemed embarrassed by the passage. He counseled prayer and masses and other devotions to dispose oneself properly.

The shortcuts philosophers have offered have not enjoyed much success. A philosopher who rejects these shortcuts, and then faces up to the many obstacles to establishing such a proof as that from motion as cogent, must wonder what the masses of men—and philosophers before they have fashioned a cogent argument of God's existence—must do. Given the manifest importance of God, if he exists, it does not seem desirable to leave the matter in limbo until a philosophical proof is had.

ORDINARY PEOPLE

Videbunt multi et timebunt et sperabunt in Domino . . .
Ps. 40:4

A feature of philosophy as it is engaged in by Thomas Aquinas and the tradition in which he stands, one that sets it off most dramatically from the main currents of modern and contemporary philosophy, is its untroubled anchoring of philosophical thought in the ordinary thinking that everybody engages in all the time. The starting points of philosophy are to be found, not by sweeping away or casting a skeptical eye on the thinking of ordinary folk, but by seeking there the well-springs of human thinking as such. The amazing assumption is that everybody already knows all sorts of things.

This will seem naive to those influenced by the hermeneutics of suspicion that has become the mark of the academic. It is as if we are constantly thanking God—if there is a God—that we are not like the rest of men. Thomas Aquinas emphasizes that it is from truths known to all

3. Pascal, *Oeuvres complètes*, 550–551.

that philosophical thinking too takes its origin. The philosopher, having reflected on their inescapable presence in his and everyone else's thinking, labels them *principia per se nota*, precepts of natural law. These labels may be unfamiliar to most people, but what they label is not. These principles are what one falls back on ultimately. They are latent in all our judgments and seldom need to be distilled from them and stated in all their elegant abstraction. When they are, they can seem the skeleton of language with the flesh removed. "A thing cannot be and not be at the same time and in the same respect." "Two things which are similar to a third thing are similar to one another." "One should do the right thing and avoid the wrong." "You shouldn't take what belongs to another." "It's wrong to get drunk." My list becomes more informative as it goes on, however abstract it still remains.

Perhaps such truths as these are only called into play when disagreements seem endless. Telling someone that a thing cannot both be and not be something or other at the same time is not the fare of ordinary discourse. Unless the circumstances are appropriate, it might even be a mark of madness to enunciate such undeniable truths. That there are twenty-six letters in the alphabet is true enough but the occasions are rare when one might want to mention this. So it is, I think, with what Thomas calls the common principles or starting points of human thinking, theoretical and practical. That is my first point: although they do not know their philosophical labels, everyone knows what is labeled by self-evident principles and first principles of practical reasoning.

My second is this. When, late in adolescence, we begin the study of logic, we are being introduced to an art that will enable us to do well what we have already been doing. Discursive thinking is synonymous with human thinking. The occurrence of "and so," "well then," "therefore" are staples of conversation. We make inferences all the time. Why logic? Because often our inferences are mistaken, and even when they are not, we may not have reflective knowledge of why this is so. Of course, logic does not help us initiate our first act of discursive thinking. It presupposes that we have been engaging in it, willy-nilly, more or less effectively, all along.

There are two kinds of philosopher: one kind denies the obvious, the other kind states the obvious. I am of the latter kind. Perhaps there is a third kind: one who simply ignores the obvious. Chesterton said that something has to be very big in order to be invisible. So too it is the most obvious that can be overlooked when it is not implicitly denied.

Nothing is more obvious than that human beings know the common principles of theoretical and practical thinking and that these truths are latent in the discursive thinking in which they are everywhere engaged. Ordinary people, untutored in logic, successively navigate from what they know to its implications all the time. That they, like philosophers, are often mistaken does not detract from the point, since the ability to recognize and correct mistakes is also part of the standard equipment of human beings.

Given these two points, can we add a third and say that ordinary folk, out of their experience of the world and themselves, come to recognize the existence of God? When St. Paul, in our favorite passage, told the Romans they could and had done this, was he addressing philosophers? Sometimes he did, of course, like those Stoics and Epicureans in Acts, but that does not seem to be the case in Romans. He seems to be saying that ordinary folk can come discursively to knowledge of the existence of God. A wag could say that the inference might take as its premise the existence of all those churches in Glasgow, but it would be an important point. Even in these twilight years of Christendom, ordinary folk may be prompted to such thoughts by the vestiges of belief that rise up architecturally around them. A former church become a theater might set our minds going. Does this muddy the water? Is the presence of religious belief an impediment to the discourse Paul speaks of? It doesn't seem so. The Romans, after all, had gods galore. Religion, pagan and Christian, Jewish or Muslim, can prompt even its adherents to discursive thinking about its fundamental presupposition.

Given the inadequacy of philosophical proofs for the existence of God, given the paucity of information they can give us, it can be expected that the term of ordinary thinking about the origin of things, of one to whom I am accountable, would, if articulated, be subject to criticism, particularly from the point of view of Christianity. Thomas Aquinas says both that it is relatively easy for people to come to knowledge of God *and* that such ordinary knowledge is woefully inadequate to its object. After all, some have thought that God is a tree. Sophisticates need not smile at this. From the point of view of faith, there is ever so much more in heaven and earth than is dreamt of in their philosophy. But that points to my next and final lecture.

FEBRUARY 17, 2000

Faith and Reason

One may define the human being, therefore, as the one who seeks the truth.

Fides et ratio, n. 28

W hile natural theology, as to its content, has its native habitat in pagan or pre-Christian philosophy, the appellation 'natural theology' has its provenance in Christianity and calls attention to the difference between the approach to God by way of natural reason, on the one hand, and by way of Revelation, on the other. In this final lecture, I would like to reflect further on this opposition.

MODI VIVENDI

From the beginning of the Christian era, thinkers have pondered the relationship between philosophical inquiry into God, his attributes, the relation between the world and God, the problem of evil, and so forth, on the one hand, and the truths about these matters which have been revealed and which are accepted as true thanks to the gift of divine faith, on the other. The Fathers of the Church, notably St. Augustine, spoke to this contrast and in what might be called the Monastic Period a *modus vivendi* was reached between faith and reason, stated in terms of the contrast between secular learning, presumed to be adequately summed up in the seven liberal arts, and sacred learning, based on Scripture. While the history of what might be called the Liberal Arts Tradition is fascinating in itself, and not as homogeneous as my remarks perhaps suggest, it did survive well into the twelfth century, when it was disturbed by the arrival in Latin translation of works of Aristotle which had hitherto been unknown. In the thirteenth century, with the foundation of universities and the possession of the Aristotelian corpus in its entirety, along with Arabic commentaries on the Aristotelian treatises, as well as many other treasures of human learning, it became clear that secular learning or philosophy and the seven liberal arts could no longer be thought of as coterminous. The university thus became the place where a new *modus vivendi* had to be worked out and, by common consent, the teaching of St. Thomas Aquinas on the matter was the most satisfying.

It was not the case, of course, that Thomas's view was accepted by all his contemporaries; indeed, during his lifetime, and afterward, his views were persistently criticized and, historically speaking, did not dominate rival positions on the relationship between faith and reason. Nonetheless, his view was to become the official view of the Church, consolidated by the Thomistic Revival inaugurated by Leo XIII in his 1879 encyclical *Aeterni Patris*. Friend and foe alike have come to take Thomas's views on this matter as either correct or the position against which to test one's steel.

Pope John Paul II in his 1998 encyclical *Faith and Reason* reviewed the history just sketched and had important things to say about the viability of the Thomistic solution today in the light of developments in philosophy. This lecture will take its departure from the thought of Thomas—as indeed many of my previous ones have—as well as from John Paul II's *Faith and Reason*.

BELIEVERS AT ODDS

Of the two diametrically opposed positions that believers may take on this matter—one holding that faith provides the only access to God and that consequently philosophical or natural theology is either a mistake or surpassed, and another that sees a complementarity of faith and reason in their approaches to God—it is the second that I shall be adopting. Earlier, in speaking of Christian philosophy, I said some few things about those believers, usually, but not always Protestants, who dismiss as presumptuous philosophical attempts to arrive at certain knowledge of God.

I shall be addressing two major questions. First, since faith is contrasted with reason in this discussion, the question arises as to the reasonableness of holding as true statements about God that one cannot demonstrate and know in that sense. Is faith a vacation from reason? Second, in the light of the impressionistic survey of the trajectory of modern philosophy given in my first set of lectures, the upshot of which was that the capacity of reason itself to attain certain truth in any area, let alone when the existence and nature of God are at issue, is called into question, it became necessary to establish the range of reason by undercutting the fundamental assumption that leads to an all too familiar contemporary skepticism. A paradoxical result of these discussions will be the realization that it has now fallen to believers to come to the defense of reason in order to defend the faith. This task is particularly urgent because of the way in which faith presupposes reason and would be unintelligible without a robust confidence in the capacity of our mind to know the world and enunciate truths about it.

The Kinds of Faith

Faith, in the sense of taking a claim to be true on the word of another, is not confined to religious matters. Our need to trust one another lies at the basis of any community. Moreover, it is often pointed out that, in the sciences, one takes as true the reports that others give of their research, without reenacting it and thereby coming to *know* that the results are true. The veracity and credibility of those engaged in any of the sciences is a necessary presupposition of advance in scientific knowledge. It was once said, with an eye to religious belief, that it is immoral to take as true anything that we do not know to be true. Of such a demand we would not simply say that it is austere, but that it is a practical impossibility. If every scientist had to *know* in the strong sense of scientific knowing everything he accepts as true within even his own narrow discipline, he would spend his life verifying the work of others and never complete the task. Nonetheless, such trust or faith among scientists is of a special kind. While it is practically impossible for the individual scientist personally to verify all that he accepts as true, it would strike us as strange to say that the whole scientific enterprise reposes on faith and thus is analogous to religious faith. The implicit *reductio* in the analogy would be that one has no more basis for objecting to religious faith than he does to the practice of the scientist. However, while it is true that it is practically impossible for a scientist to verify personally *everything* that he holds as scientifically true, it is possible for him to verify personally *anything* he holds as scientifically true. Indeed, that is the implicit assumption of his trust. He believes a scientific claim to be true in the sense that he believes that he or any other competent scientist could show it is true. In this his faith is very different from religious faith. The Trinity is not an hypothesis that I or anyone else could show to be true.

But if the faith of scientists is thus markedly different from religious faith, the interpersonal trust of human beings is not always or obviously a matter of verifiable truths. Indeed, the activity of scientists might seem to be a peculiarly regional instance of our trust in one another and scarcely paradigmatic of it. Most of the things we trust one another about are not expressible as claims whose truth is attainable independently of the relationship between one person and another. A promise is a commitment to make something true. When a man and woman marry they "plight one another their troth." They are not predicting that something or other will be the case in five, ten, or fifty years; rather, they pledge to make it the case, in sickness and in health, in good times and bad. How could they *know* they are putting themselves in good hands? They could not know it with anything resembling scientific knowledge, of course, and yet they do know it. This kind of interpersonal trust is a far better analogue to religious belief.

NEMO CREDIT NISI VOLENS

Thomas Aquinas discusses the act of religious faith in terms of Augustine's definition of it as *"cum assensione cogitare: thinking with assent."* Thinking may be either simple or complex, thinking of a thing, which could be expressed in a definition, or thinking something about it, which would be expressed in a proposition. Only propositions are true or false and of any proposition it can be said that either it or its contradictory is true. Complex thinking thus takes place under the sign

$p \lor \sim p$. But which? When we are in a state of doubt, we vacillate between contradictories and assent to neither. When we have an opinion, we choose one of contradictories but do not assent to it in such a way that we wholly exclude the possibility that its opposite is true: the evidence is not conclusive. When we wholly exclude the other contradictory, we are said to assent. But this can come about either thanks to intellect or to will. *Thanks to intellect*, when the terms of the proposition are such that we immediately assent to it, as to something self-evident. But when a proposition is not self-evident, we may nonetheless give it our full assent because it follows demonstratively from true and necessary premises. *Thanks to will*, when the mind settles on one of contradictories, not because it is compelled to do so because of self-evidence or because it has been demonstrated, but because the will prompts assent to the good involved in so assenting.[1] In this way, we can trust another person in the interpersonal way described above. And in this way too we believe in the religious sense.

Whatever thinking is done about what is proposed for our belief, it cannot bring the mind to assent because what is proposed is self-evident or follows necessarily from other things we know to be true. The thinking (*cogitatio*) does not cause assent (*assensus*), as it does in the case of demonstration. What enables the mind to give its assent to revealed truth is the fact that the will under the influence of grace is moved by the promise of an eternal happiness, which is the reward for the assent. Because the mind is moved by will and not by the evidence of the object, the assent does not stop the mind from continued pondering (*cogitatio*).

Sed in fide est assensus et cogitatio quasi ex aequo: non enim assensus ex cogitatione causatur sed ex voluntate, ut dictum est; sed quia intellectus non hoc modo terminatur ad unum ut ad proprium terminum perducatur, qui est visio alicuius intelligibilis, inde est quod eius motus nondum est quietatus, sed adhuc habet cogitationem et inquisitionem

In faith assent and cogitation are present equally, for the assent is not caused by cogitation but by will, as has been said; and since intellect is not thus terminated to one [of contradictories] as when it is brought to its proper term, which is the seeing of something intelligible, so its activity is not yet at rest, but cogitation and inquiry

1. "... determinatur autem per voluntatem quae elegit assentire uni parti determinate et praecise propter aliquid quod est sufficiens ad movendum voluntatem non autem ad

de his qui credit quamvis eis firmissime assentiat: quantum enim est ex se ipso non est ei satisfactum nec est terminatus ad unum sed terminatur tantum ex extrinsico. (*Q.D. de veritate*, q. 14, a. 1, c.)

continue concerning what one believes, even though he most firmly assents to it: taken as such, [intellect] is not satisfied nor is it terminated in one, except by an extrinsic cause.

It will be seen how close this account of faith is to Kierkegaard's discussion of subjective truth: "An objective uncertainty held fast in an appropriation process of the most passionate inwardness." And one can see too why Cardinal Newman insisted that the considerations that led to his acceptance of the Catholic faith were probabilities, not conclusive reasoning. But for all their probable character, the upshot was a firm and certain assent.

PHILOSOPHY AND THEOLOGY

Knowing and believing being distinguished in this way, one can go on to speak of philosophy and theology. As we have argued earlier, the philosopher takes his beginnings from truths which are the common possession of mankind. He reflects on these and labels them as we suggested, and then goes on in pursuit of further knowledge, which may take him very far indeed from the concerns of ordinary human beings. For all that, he shares with them from first to last the common truths which serve as his principles. The truths of faith are the possession of all believers, but the theologian reflects on them, using the more or less sophisticated techniques he has learned in his previous studies. It was the hallmark of Scholastic theology that it brought to the pondering of the truths of faith techniques learned while studying philosophy, most particularly that of Aristotle.[2] The theologian will accordingly ask what

---

movendum intellectum, utpote quia videtur bonum vel conveniens huic parti assentire; et ista est dispositio credentis ut cum aliquis credit dictis alicuius hominis quia videtur decens vel utile. Et sic etiam movemur ad credendum dictis Dei in quantum nobis repromittitur, si crediderimus, praemium aeternae vitae; et hoc praemio movetur voluntas ad assentiendum his quae dicuntur quamvis intellectus non moveatur per aliquid intellectum: et ideo dicit Augustinus quod 'cetera potest homo nolens, credere non nisi volens'" (*Q. D. de veritate*, q. 14, a. 1, c.).

2. See John I. Jenkins, C.S.C., *Knowledge and Faith in Thomas Aquinas* (Cambridge: Cambridge University Press, 1997).

the subject of his discipline is, what the principles of his science are, what proofs are appropriate to it, and he will go on—if he is Thomas Aquinas—to construct a vast and complicated intellectual edifice setting out the faith by ordering its contents, developing the implications of believed truths, and ways of handling those who attack the faith. *Fides quaerens intellectum.* The truths of faith are to theology as the common principles are to philosophy. However similar to philosophical discourse theological discourse might look, the essential and abiding difference lies in their starting points. Just as the philosopher assumes, along with everybody else, the truth of the common principles and goes on from there, so the theologian assumes the truths of the faith, along with all other believers, and goes on from there. The structure of theological discourse can look very much like that of philosophy, but the whole edifice depends on truths accepted on the basis of faith. That is, truths not known to be true, but believed.

THE REASONABLENESS
OF FAITH

Given the character of theology and the background of the theologian, the question of how the act of reason that is believing compares to the act of reason that is knowing is bound to be raised. Is it reasonable to give assent to truths one cannot understand? The reasonableness of faith cannot be shown by proving that the propositions which express its object are true. It is however possible to argue, as we showed at the end of Lecture Five, that the assent of faith is reasonable. That argument is based on a difference that is noted among the truths that have been revealed and which are thus accepted on faith. Among them are to be found truths about God—that he is one, that he is the cause of all else, etc.—which have been established by pagan philosophers, that is, independently of revelation and faith. Most of what has been revealed is unknowable in this life, however. The first subset of revealed truths was dubbed *praeambula fidei,* and the second larger subset *mysteria fidei.* Because of this, faith sometimes bears on a truth that is knowable, and some believers, thanks to argument, may come to see the truth of the preambles. The reasonableness of believing consists in this: that, if some of what has been revealed can be known to be intelligible and true, it is reasonable to accept the rest as intelligible and true.

The reasonableness of faith is also seen in the way the believer refutes objections to the faith. Such a refutation takes many forms. A charge that the believer is assenting to something that is obviously unintelligible will be met by an argument showing it is not obviously unintelligible. Thus, refutation takes the form of showing that the arguments against the faith are not conclusive, however probable they may be. And the believer concedes that sometimes they seem very probable. Refutations or responses of this kind must take care not to seem to show that the contradictory of a mystery of the faith is necessarily false. If one knows that one of contradictories is false, one knows that the other—in this case the mystery—is true. Sometimes the believer must content himself with showing that if the naysayer were right, he would have to be equally critical of something he presumably would not wish to be. This kind of argument has been developed into a fine art by my colleague Al Plantinga.

THE ASYMMETRY OF FAITH AND KNOWLEDGE

One who has been brought up in the faith accepts as true a vast number of truths about God, many of them implicitly—he accepts whatever God has revealed—but in his frequent recitation of the Creed he will articulate the most important of them. Among the articles, or presupposed by them, are truths about God that philosophers, pagan and otherwise, have established on the basis of proof. When the theologian calls these "preambles of faith," he is calling attention to their presence within Revelation. He might even say that the mysteries of faith entail the preambles of faith.[3] This inclusion of truths which can be established by reason within the deposit of faith, and the fact that faith provides the principles of theology, can suggest that philosophy is thereby assumed into theology and the distinction between the two disciplines overcome.

---

3. It would be misleading in the extreme to understand "preambles" to mean that the believer advances from them to the mysteries of the faith. He accepts all of them at once and under the same formality, because they have been revealed by God. Etienne Gilson was particularly vexed by the suggestion that natural theology was a necessary prelude to the faith, as if the believer, qua believer, had first to prove the existence of God and then go on to the Incarnation and Trinity. See *Le philosophe et la théologie* (Paris: Fayard, 1960).

But the *praeambula fidei* are not as such the whole of philosophy, unless one maintains that in order to establish their truth the whole of philosophy is required, since truths about God fall to metaphysics which is the culmination of the philosophical task, the wisdom out of desire for which one began. Gilson gave as the subject matter of Christian philosophy the *praeambula fidei*. Theology, though not faith, presupposes philosophy, and thus the establishment of naturally knowable truths about God would come prior to taking up the task of theology.

If, seen as part of the deposit of faith, the acquisitions of natural theology are seen as preambulatory to what is of faith in the strong sense,[4] it should not be thought that they in any way entail the mysteries or compel one to believe. The preambles may be entailed by, be implicit in, the *mysteria* the believer believes. But what is of faith is neither entailed by nor implicit in what can be known about God by natural reason. This asymmetry between faith and reason allays the fears of those believers who consider natural theology to be but a first step on a path that leads as well to making the mysteries claims whose truth can be decided by the usual philosophical methods.

THREE VERSIONS OF PHILOSOPHY

In his encyclical *Faith and Reason*, John Paul II distinguishes two different stances of philosophy vis-à-vis Christian faith: first, a *philosophy completely independent of the Gospel's Revelation*. This was the case perforce of the pagan philosophers in the pre-Christian era. "We see here philosophy's valid aspiration to be an *autonomous* enterprise, obeying its own rules and employing the powers of reason alone" (n. 75). Although it is a search for truth within the natural order—it knew no other—as a search for truth, pagan philosophy "is always open—at least implicitly—to the supernatural" (ibid.). In the Christian era, the autonomy of philosophy must be respected "even when theological discourse makes use of philosophical concepts and arguments." This autonomy is explained by the fact that arguments according to rig-

---

4. Only the *mysteria* are strictly speaking objects of faith, since the only way they can be held as true is on divine authority; the *praeambula*, while no doubt believed by most, can in principle be known and thus for them to be believed is *per accidens* to them.

orous rational criteria are meant to arrive at results that are "universally valid." Presumably this distinguishes philosophical arguments from theological since the latter are seen to be truth-bearing only by those who have faith, that is, hold as true the principles of theology. He goes on to distinguish autonomy from separation, "This theory claims for philosophy not only a valid autonomy, but a self-sufficiency of thought which is patently invalid. In refusing the truth offered by divine Revelation, philosophy only does itself damage, since this is to preclude access to a deeper knowledge of truth" (ibid.). It is safe to say that such a statement would raise the hackles of the majority of professional philosophers. But the contrast is prelude to the notion of Christian philosophy. Thus, what the pope called a first stance of philosophy toward Christian faith turns out to be two, either one in which the philosopher is wholly unaware of Christianity and goes about his work, or one in which the philosopher, being aware of Christianity, dismisses it on the basis that reason is sufficient unto itself, and thus excludes Christianity. The discussion of Christian philosophy, on this reading, turns out to be a third possible stance.

The pope distinguishes two aspects of Christian philosophy, a subjective and an objective. One subjective effect of the faith on the philosopher is to bring home to him that, however great the reach of reason, there is a vast reality beyond the grasp of our understanding. He will also supplement what he can know with what he believes in discussing such vexed questions as the problem of evil and suffering, the personal nature of God, the meaning of life, and why is there anything at all rather than nothing. There is here a mixture of the influence of virtues on the believer and the claim that the data of Revelation are helpful in handling some difficult philosophical questions. When he turns to the objective side of Christian philosophy, there is therefore an overlap. Under the influence of their faith, philosophers have clarified God's causality and his personal nature. The notion of sin has influenced their philosophical discussions of evil. And the notion of person is perhaps one of the most obvious philosophical benefits under the influence of faith. But the further menu of topics that fall to Christian philosophy—the rationality of certain truths expressed in Scripture, the possibility of man's supernatural vocation—does not pertain to philosophy. "In speculating on these questions, philosophers have not become theologians, since they have not sought to understand and expound the truths of faith on the basis of Revelation" (n. 76). But will they presume to understand and expound the faith on the basis of rational principles? The discussion of Christian philosophy seems to merge into the following discussion of philosophy as the *ancilla theologiae*, the theologian's use of philosophy.

THE CHRISTIAN PHILOSOPHER

For some believers their one intellect is the subject not only of the virtue of faith but also of such intellectual virtues as science, metaphysics, and the like. That there should be commerce between what he believes and what he knows is unsurprising; he is after all but one person. Personally, subjectively, his intellectual life must seem a continuum, with matters of faith as familiar to him as Goedel's Theorem. On reflection, he realizes the different provenance of truths of faith and philosophical truths, and this will perhaps prompt an explicit consideration of their difference. Any such comparison must be thought of as theological, since it is discourse within the ambit of revealed truths which are the guide, and are not the upshot, of the discussion. The believing philosopher will doubtless be guided in his discussion of evil by what he holds on the basis of his faith, but the latter will not be thematic in the philosophical discussion as such. If he mentions the role Christ's Passion plays in his understanding of the seriousness of evil, his non-believing colleague will understand that nothing strictly of faith can be crucial in the argument as philosophical. The believer does not wish to redefine the nature of philosophy; on the contrary, he insists on its difference from theology. But in his practice he will be a constant rebuke and irritant to those who wish to ply the philosophical trade in total separation from, indeed in more or less explicit opposition, to Christianity. Philosopher after philosopher in recent times has defined knowledge or truth or meaning in such a way as explicitly to exclude Christian faith as reasonable. It is modern philosophy, in other words, that has thus injected theology into philosophical discussions. Perhaps only when it is considered as lapsed Christian philosophy will we understand the animus of modern thought against Christian faith. In any case, on both sides, the discussions will not remain within the limits of philosophy as traditionally understood. Unmasked as theologians *manqués*, the great figures of modern and contemporary philosophy will be seen as themselves warranting the placement of philosophical discussions in the wider context of Christianity. What has been called the Atheology of modern philosophy is, after all, often a theological excursion.

IN DEFENSE OF REASON

Perhaps the most striking aspect of *Faith and Reason* is its defense of reason. *Mirabile dictu,* the encyclical's survey of the trajectory of modern philosophy reaches a conclusion not unlike that reached in my October lectures. The search for truth has given way to pragmatic compromises based on the epistemological assumption that the mind is incapable of grasping a reality which would render its judgments true. But a mind incapable of the truth is not an apt subject for Christian faith. That is why the encyclical makes its plea for philosophers to get back to work with a renewed confidence that the work can be done. It asks philosophy to "verify the human capacity to *know the truth,* to come to a knowledge which can reach objective truth by means of that *adaequatio rei et intellectus* to which the Scholastic Doctors referred" (n. 82). That this is a presupposition of faith is a powerful stimulus to the believing philosopher to devote himself to the defense of reason.

ADIEU

In these lectures I have tried, in a modest way, to clear away some obstacles to carrying on the noble work of philosophy. These are times in which doubt is cast on our ability to know anything at all, let alone that God exists. This creates special difficulties for one whose task it was to discuss natural theology. Much of what I have had to say, accordingly, is preliminary, for it seemed to me that, without some effort, however inadequate, to remove the obstacles that have been placed in the path of our pursuit of truth, it would have been impossible to even gesture in the direction of the recovery of natural theology. So mine has been, perforce, a modest task, modestly performed, but for all that of fundamental importance.

FEBRUARY 22, 2000

Index